PRAISE FOR *A NATION OF IMMIGRANTS*

"President Kennedy understood that the story of America is, above all else, the story of immigrants. In this timeless book, he shows how the United States has always been enriched by the steady flow of men, women, and families to our shores. It is a reminder that America's best leaders have embraced, not feared, the diversity which makes America great. As a proud American immigrant, I am grateful that this book has been republished and hopeful that new generations will learn from President Kennedy's wisdom on this vital issue."

—Former Secretary of State Madeleine K. Albright

"*A Nation of Immigrants* is an enduring reminder of where we—the United States of America—come from. We must remain mindful that there is much more that unites us than divides us—the shared values of family, the dignity of work, the hope for upward mobility, and freedom from oppression and persecution. John F. Kennedy's legacies are many but let *A Nation of Immigrants* always remind us of our shared dreams, goals, and destiny as a nation."

—U.S. Senator Marco Rubio

"This reissue of President John F. Kennedy's thoughtful essay on immigration in America—its origins, its benefits, and the challenges to it—is incredibly timely. Reading *A Nation of Immigrants* should invigorate us all as we fight the forces of fear and hatred that seek to end all immigration to this country. President Kennedy's discussion of the 'American philosophy of equality,' which draws people here from all over the globe, and his survey of the successes and contributions of each generation of newcomers remind us of the power of immigrants to build and improve our country. 'Immigration,' he tells us, 'is . . . the expression in action of a positive belief in the possibility of a better life.' As an immigrant to this country, I know that first hand. In these times, which are not normal, it is incumbent on us to spread this belief and ensure that America is able to benefit from many more generations of immigrant families to come."

—Senator Mazie K. Hirono

"President Kennedy, in his timeless book on immigration, reminds us of the fact that we are a nation of immigrants. This book makes it clear that

through the course of our history, immigrants have made significant contributions to shape the America we know today. The words are more relevant and important today than when it was [first] published. The debate on immigration will be informed by the history and significance of immigration to creating the fabric of the country we know and love."
—U.S. Senator Mel Martínez (FL Retired)

"The United States has benefited incalculably from the richly diverse perspectives and entrepreneurial contributions of immigrants and refugees whose hands have helped to form our nation. Their legacy has ignited arguably the most enterprising spirit and innovative culture in the history of our world. President Kennedy related this greatness in a timeless essay that describes the uniqueness of our pluralistic democracy—the product of the energy and ingenuity of those we have welcomed to our shores—and that serves as a worthy reminder for our times."
—Daniel Lubetzky, founder and CEO of KIND Healthy Snacks

"Written in 1958, *A Nation of Immigrants* is every bit as relevant today as it was when written 60 years ago. Then Senator Kennedy's thesis is still valid today that, while America has struggled since our founding with fear of the other and with reforming our immigration laws, our nation has benefitted as much from immigrants as immigrants have benefitted from joining our nation. A nation of immigrants."
—Mark Hetfield, president and CEO, HIAS (founded in 1881 as the Hebrew Immigrant Aid Society)

"Sixty years later, President Kennedy's *A Nation of Immigrants* remains one of the purest descriptions of the promise of America. Rarely has a message been more timeless and more timely. Kennedy's honest assessment of the challenges and opportunities of immigration is more than a take on our history. It is a roadmap for how our nation's leaders should represent and advance American values."
—Ali Noorani, executive director, National Immigration Forum

"Kennedy's eloquent account of the contributions and sacrifices made by legions of prior immigrants to build and nurture this great nation is a potent—and timely—reminder that there is strength in difference and power in diversity."
—Joichi Ito, director of the MIT Media Lab

A NATION OF IMMIGRANTS

ALSO BY JOHN F. KENNEDY

The Burden and the Glory
(edited by Allan Nevins)

To Turn the Tide
(edited by John W. Gardner)

The Strategy of Peace
(edited by Allan Nevins)

Profiles in Courage

Why England Slept

A
NATION
OF
IMMIGRANTS

JOHN F. KENNEDY

HARPER**PERENNIAL** ● MODERN**CLASSICS**

NEW YORK ● LONDON ● TORONTO ● SYDNEY ● NEW DELHI ● AUCKLAND

HARPER**PERENNIAL** ● MODERN**CLASSICS**

A hardcover edition of this book was published in 1964 by Harper & Row, Publishers.

HarperCollins books may be purchased for educational, business, or sales promotional use. For information, please email the Special Markets Department at SPsales@harpercollins.com.

FIRST HARPER PERENNIAL EDITION PUBLISHED 2008.

FIRST UPDATED HARPER PERENNIAL MODERN CLASSICS EDITION PUBLISHED 2018.

ISBN: 978-0-06-285969-3

Designed by Jamie Lynn Kerner

Library of Congress Cataloging-in-Publication Data has been applied for.

23 24 25 26 27 LBC 10 9 8 7 6

CONTENTS

FOREWORD

THE ANTI-DEFAMATION LEAGUE (ADL) HAS HUMBLE beginnings, but it has always been powered by a timeless and influential purpose. Back in 1913 when the organization was founded, our entire operation was little more than a desk in a small law firm. Today, we have 25 locations spread across North America, including our main office on the tenth floor of a tall glass-and-steel skyscraper in midtown Manhattan.

Though the size of our organization has changed much over the past century, our core mission remains unchanged, encoded into the DNA of the organization: "to stop the defamation of the Jewish people, and to secure justice and fair treatment to all."

Just about every day, I am reminded of the power of this mission—and the impact ADL has had over the past century.

Hanging on the wall of my office, matted in a gold frame, is a pen, notecard, and Western Union telegram on weathered paper. The telegram was sent by Lawrence O'Brien, special assistant to President Lyndon Johnson, to former ADL National Director Ben Epstein inviting him to a bill-signing ceremony that would take place on October 3, 1965. The law that was being signed was the Immigration and Nationality Act of 1965, the landmark piece of legislation that ushered in the most diverse wave of new Americans since the United States was founded approximately 200 years earlier.

Ben received this telegram—and took home one of the pens that LBJ used to sign the act—because of the bold role that ADL had taken to champion immigration reform based on our own history and compelled by our mission. Long before it was a cause celebre, before nationwide rallies and online petitions, ADL had launched a deliberate and determined campaign of advocacy that began with one simple spark.

This book.

Its origins trace back to the mid-1950s when ADL leadership, alarmed by rising xenophobia and anti-immigrant fervor, saw the echoes of an earlier pattern. At numerous points in prior decades, America had closed its doors to people fleeing prejudice, discrimination, and violence. In the early 1900s, these were Jews exiting czarist Russia, seeking a life free from pogroms. In the 1930s, these were Jews escaping Germany and neighboring countries during the brutality of the Third Reich. In the 1940s, these were Jews fleeing the graveyards of Europe and hoping to find a safer and more stable existence.

In the 1950s, Jews were not the main group that sought refuge, but the recent trauma of their own refugee experience had scarred the American Jewish community and its institutions, including Ben. So, he reached out to a young junior senator from the Commonwealth of Massachusetts, and asked him to write a book that explained our diverse American roots to the ill-informed, reminding them that the

United States is a country of refugees and a nation of immigrants. That senator was John F. Kennedy.

Kennedy delivered on this request, but also did more. He concluded his essay with his vision for immigration reform, particularly the elimination of the national origins quota system, a bold idea that makes the book especially timely. As we know, JFK tragically was assassinated before the passage of the 1965 Act that the book helped to inspire. But the legislation signed by that pen hanging in my office converted his idea into the law of the land and changed the shape of our country for the better.

For me, the book and its lofty ideals are not some abstract history lesson. It's literally real life. My life.

My paternal grandfather came to the United States on a ship in 1938. Bernard Greenblatt was a young man who once lived freely in Germany as did a large number of highly educated and successful Jews. There was a degree of anti-Jewish bias, but it did not impede their lives. Moreover, his father fought in World War I so their patriotism could not be questioned—or so he thought. The rise of Hitler changed all that as anti-Semitism burst out into the open and the onset of the Nuremberg Laws that codified casual prejudice into legislated hate.

My grandfather escaped with falsified travel documents—because Jews were not permitted to leave—when he made his way to America from Germany via France. He was registered as a refugee and eventually obtained citizenship. In the ensuing years, he carved out a middle-class life for himself and his family, including my father, on the East Coast.

Interestingly, almost 50 years later, my wife and her family came to this country under similar conditions. They fled the oppressive policies of the Islamic Republic of Iran, a theocratic government that came to power via the violent overthrow of the Shah of Iran. Led by Ayatollah Khomeini, the new government exhibited tremendous hostility toward secularism that was complemented by a virulent antipathy toward religious minorities. Despite a thousand-year presence of Jews in Iran, the regime targeted them for high-profile executions and imposed a wave of new restrictions, such as forcing Jewish girls and women to wear hijabs and to abide by the same Islamic restrictions that they imposed on the general population.

My wife and her family escaped with falsified travel documents because, well, Jews were not permitted to emigrate. They fled their homeland via France, eventually making their way to America. They were registered as political refugees and eventually obtained citizenship. In the ensuing years, the family carved out a middle-class life on the West Coast.

Interestingly, these stories are far from unique. In fact, there are many echoes if you listen to others' stories.

You can hear those echoes when you talk to the Punjabi Sikh family that came to America, escaping the terrible pain of partition in post-colonial India. You can hear them when you talk to the Vietnamese families who fled their homeland in the wake of the terrible violence of the eponymous war and its aftermath. You can hear them when you talk to Venezuelan families who bolted from their country in light of the dictatorial policies of Hugo Chavez and his successors. You can hear them when you talk to the Iraqi and Syrian families who endeavored to escape the catastrophic violence that leveled their countries, mayhem typically wrought by Sunni Jihadists in terror organizations like ISIS or Al Qaeda or their Shiite counterparts such as Hezbollah or foreign militias funded by Iran. And you can hear them today at the southern border of the United States among migrants from Central and South America, facing the tragic separation from their children, often leaving family members behind to escape oppression and to seek opportunity.

But whether America served as a refuge to those escaping violence or a haven for those simply seeking a better life, our country traditionally has been an inspiration to others, a place that offered hope to the hopeless and opportunity to the downtrodden.

In recent times, however, we have seen an increase in rhetoric across the country that does not promote the ideals of our democracy. Today, we face a global refugee crisis of epic proportions, the largest since World War II. Images and stories of the worst kind of suffering and misery have evoked compassion in many quarters, but also have prompted some to try to shut our borders rather than open them to the most needy among us. It is a stark departure from JFK's vision and from the words of Emma Lazarus, who wrote the poetry on the pedestal of Lady Liberty.

This book reminds us that immigration is a cornerstone of our glorious history and truly has enabled the America of our modern age. And there could be no better person to have written these words than President Kennedy. His own life exemplified some of our most cherished values—courage, service, patriotism, and integrity.

It reminds us that, to paraphrase Martin Luther King Jr., American history is not an arc that organically angles in a more moral direction simply due to the forces of nature. Rather, the arc of history can meander in any multitude of directions. In fact, it is up to us to bend the arc of history, not with our will, but with our actions and with our very souls. Our revolutionary creed reminds us that we have the power to shape the outcome if we seize the moment and create the outcome that we seek. This was a fact that Ben Epstein profoundly understood. And this book was but one of the many ways that President Kennedy bent the arc of history in a more humane direction.

It was an act of courage when ADL published this book in 1958. It helped to shape the conversation of the time and shape our country's history. Hopefully, it can shape both of them again in our own time. And so it is an act of gratitude that we republish *A Nation of Immigrants* 60 years after it was written to lift up its message at a moment when it seems more relevant than ever.

—Jonathan Greenblatt, CEO and national director of ADL

INTRODUCTION

by Congressman Joe Kennedy III

MY FATHER HAS A MEMORY OF MY GREAT-GRANDMOTHER Rose that he shares from time to time. He was outside playing with his sister Kathleen one day when she called them back home. She led them to a small room and dug out a big photo album. My dad was sure that she was going to make them sit there and go through old family photos for hours. A young boy at the time, he squirmed and looked longingly out the window at his Cape Cod summer day.

But Grandma Rose quickly flipped to the very back of the album and pulled out a stack of carefully folded, faded newspapers. One after another, she opened them up to the Help Wanted section. There, she handed him ad after ad marked with big block letters: NO IRISH NEED APPLY.

Her message was clear: This is where you came from. This is who you are. This is the pain, sweat, and tears that generations before you bore, so you would never feel the sting of prejudice. And this is the responsibility you inherit today.

For generations of my family, immigration reform became a personal fight. Few felt it as deeply as President John F. Kennedy. In the pages to come, my great-uncle outlines the compelling case for immigration, in economic, moral, and global terms. "The abundant resources of this land provided the foundation for a great nation," he writes. "But only people could make the opportunity a reality. Immigration provided the human resources." Cultivating, challenging, and caring for that most precious resource became the cause of his life.

Two months after his election, President Kennedy came home to Boston to deliver his farewell address to Massachusetts. In a nod to the words of John Winthrop and the plight of those who first took the perilous journey to our shores, he echoed the expectations that have become synonymous with the American name. "Today the eyes of all people are truly upon us," he said, "and our governments, in every branch, at every level . . . must be as a city upon a hill, constructed and inhabited by men aware of their great trust and their great responsibility."

Eighteen years later, another president would summon the words of Winthrop in his farewell address to the American people:

"I've spoken of the shining city all my political life, but I don't know if I ever quite communicated what I saw when I said it," said Ronald Reagan. "But in my mind it was a tall, proud city built on rocks stronger than oceans, windswept, God-blessed, and teeming with people of all kinds living in harmony and peace; a city with free ports that hummed with commerce and creativity. And if there had to be city walls, the walls had doors and the doors were open to anyone with the will and the heart to get here."

In moments of great reflection, transition, and vulnerability, great men saw the American story not through the lens of politics or tribe. They saw it as it surely looked to John Winthrop and every weary traveler who has ever approached American shores—rocky, imperfect, and unknown, but expansive, limitless, and defiantly hopeful.

Since the beginning, immigration has been an *affirmation* of our success, not a threat to it. People risk everything to reach this land because they believe in our greatness—our fair laws, our good values, our promises and possibilities. We should not worry when the striving and suffering arrive on our shores; we should worry when they stop coming at all.

Today that legacy—our legacy—is being threatened, by the same chorus that met President Kennedy when he had the boldness to tackle the racialized quota system. Their voices sound familiar: *Immigrants will flood our cities and towns. They will take our jobs. They will threaten our culture. They aren't from here. They aren't like us.*

Fifty years later, those voices still have not updated their talking points. Fifty years later, our broken immigration system is still a source of oppression, of anguish, and of loss.

As I write this today, thousands of immigrant children remain separated from their parents on American soil. They showed up at our border terrorized, desperate, and afraid. And in an act of unimaginable brutality, our government responded with terror of its own—taking infants and toddlers out of their families' arms.

This is the human wreckage of American immigration policy. This is the trauma and torture that dark forces of nativism, supremacy, and prejudice have brought to bear in a land that staked its name on brighter, better things: equality, dignity and freedom.

This is the work that lies ahead, daunting and dangerous, but familiar, as President Kennedy reminds us in the pages that follow. We have been here before. We have spent generations battling those who would make America sharp and small and scared. We have risen, we have challenged, we have dragged ourselves toward a more perfect union.

We have done that by seeing a little of ourselves, our history, and our experience in others' eyes. By choosing compassion and mercy and grace—not just because they are right, but because they are smart. Because we are richer and stronger and freer when we aim for less suffering, less trauma, less poverty, less prejudice.

There's a great story that makes its way around Irish-American quarters here in Boston. In the midst of the Great Hunger in Ireland, the Choctaw Indian tribe of Oklahoma heard about the plight of the Irish; read about starving women and children dying along the roads, their mouths stained green with the grass they ate in desperate search of nourishment.

They collected $170 and sent it to Ireland for famine relief, mindful of their own struggles and the Trail of Tears that had led them less than 20 years earlier to their new home in Indian Territory. From the painful lessons of their own past, they were called to help people they didn't know, who looked different, spoke different, were different. But who suffered just the same.

Today we summon that example. We summon the feelings of fear, loss, desperation, and isolation that visit each of us in different ways no matter our privilege or protection. In that shared humanity we find our empathy. We find our strength. We find the proud and dusty pages of our story that prove ours is a country unafraid to open, extend, and expand. We find our voices—like the hundreds of thousands of Americans who have risen up in response to the current immigration policies and said: *No. Not on my land. Not in my name.*

They have donated money and time and skills to reunite broken families. They have fostered young children left alone on our shores. They have taken to the streets and the courts, state legislatures and halls of Congress, to demand something better, fairer, kinder, and stronger from the government that represents them.

President Kennedy would be proud. It is the call not just to action but to decency that echoes through these pages. It is the confident, charismatic country he believed in. Most important, it is the simple Gospel he knew would bind us to each other through time and space and generations—no matter creed or country, color or class.

"For I was hungry and you gave me food, I was thirsty and you gave me drink, *I was a stranger and you welcomed me.*"

A NATION OF IMMIGRANTS

CHAPTER 1

A NATION OF NATIONS

ON MAY 11, 1831, ALEXIS DE TOCQUEVILLE, A YOUNG French aristocrat, disembarked in the bustling harbor of New York City. He had crossed the ocean to try to understand the implications for European civilization of the new experiment in democracy on the far side of the Atlantic. In the next nine months, Tocqueville and his friend Gustave de Beaumont traveled the length and breadth of the eastern half of the continent—from Boston to Green Bay and from New Orleans to Quebec—in search of the essence of American life.

Tocqueville was fascinated by what he saw. He marveled at the energy of the people who were building the new nation. He admired many of the new political institutions and ideals. And he was impressed most of all by the spirit of equality that pervaded the life and customs of the people. Though he had reservations about some of the expressions of this spirit, he could discern its workings in every aspect of American society—in politics, business, personal relations, culture, thought. This commitment to equality was in striking contrast to the class-ridden society of Europe. Yet Tocqueville believed "the democratic revolution" to be irresistible.

"Balanced between the past and the future," as he wrote of himself, "with no natural instinctive attraction toward either, I could without effort quietly contemplate each side of the question." On his return to France, Tocqueville delivered his dispassionate and penetrating judgment of the American experiment in his great work *Democracy in America*. No one, before or since, has written about the United States with such insight. And, in discussing the successive waves of immigration from England, France, Spain and other European countries, Tocqueville identified a central factor in the American democratic faith:

> All these European colonies contained the elements, if not the development, of a complete democracy. Two causes led to this result. It may be said that on leaving the mother country the emigrants had, in general, no notion of superiority one over another. The happy and powerful do not go into exile, and there are no surer guarantees of equality among men than poverty and misfortune.

To show the power of the equalitarian spirit in America, Tocqueville added: "It happened, however, on several occasions, that persons of rank were driven to America by political and religious quarrels. Laws were made to establish a gradation of ranks; but it was soon found that the soil of America was opposed to a territorial aristocracy."

What Alexis de Tocqueville saw in America was a society of immigrants, each of whom had begun life anew, on an equal footing. This was the secret of America: a nation of people with the fresh memory of old traditions who dared to explore new frontiers, people eager to build lives for themselves in a spacious society that did not restrict their freedom of choice and action.

Since 1607, when the first English settlers reached the New World, over 42 million people have migrated to the United States. This represents the largest migration of people in all recorded history. It is two and a half times the total number of people now living in Arizona, Arkansas, Colorado, Delaware, Idaho, Kansas, Maine, Montana, Nevada, New Hampshire, New Mexico, North Dakota, Oregon, Rhode Island, South Dakota, Utah, Vermont and Wyoming.

Another way of indicating the importance of immigration to America is to point out that every American who ever lived, with the exception of one group, was either an immigrant himself or a descendant of immigrants.

The exception? Will Rogers, part Cherokee Indian, said that his ancestors were at the dock to meet the *Mayflower*. And some anthropologists believe that the Indians themselves were immigrants from another continent who displaced the original Americans—the aborigines.

In just over 350 years, a nation of nearly 200 million people has grown up, populated almost entirely by persons who either came from other lands or whose forefathers came from other lands. As President Franklin D. Roosevelt reminded a convention of the Daughters of the American Revolution, "Remember, remember always, that all of us, and you and I especially, are descended from immigrants and revolutionists."

Any great social movement leaves its mark, and the massive migration of peoples to the New World was no exception to this rule. The interaction of disparate cultures, the vehemence of the ideals that led the immigrants here, the opportunity offered by a new life, all gave America a flavor and a character that make it as unmistakable and as remarkable to people today as it was to Alexis de Tocqueville in the early part of the nineteenth century. The contribution of immigrants can be seen in every aspect of our national life. We see it in religion, in politics, in business, in the arts, in education, even in athletics and in entertainment. There is no part of our nation that has not been touched by our immigrant background. Everywhere immigrants have enriched and strengthened the fabric of American life. As Walt Whitman said,

> *These States are the amplest poem,*
> *Here is not merely a nation but*
> *a teeming Nation of nations.*

To know America, then, it is necessary to understand this peculiarly American social revolution. It is necessary to know why over 42 million people gave up their settled lives to start anew in a strange land. We must know how they met the new land and how it met them, and, most important, we must know what these things mean for our present and for our future.

CHAPTER 2

WHY THEY CAME

LITTLE IS MORE EXTRAORDINARY THAN THE DECISION to migrate, little more extraordinary than the accumulation of emotions and thoughts which finally leads a family to say farewell to a community where it has lived for centuries, to abandon old ties and familiar landmarks, and to sail across dark seas to a strange land. Today, when mass communications tell one part of the world all about another, it is relatively easy to understand how poverty or tyranny might compel people to exchange an old nation for a new one. But centuries ago migration was a leap into the unknown. It was an enormous intellectual and emotional commitment. The forces that moved our forebears to their great decision—the decision to leave their homes and begin an adventure filled with incalculable uncertainty, risk and hardship—must have been of overpowering proportions.

Oscar Handlin, in his book *The Uprooted,* describes the experience of the immigrants:

The crossing immediately subjected the emigrant to a succession of shattering shocks and decisively conditioned the life of every man that survived it. This was the initial contact with life as it was to be. For many peasants it was the first time away from home, away from the safety of the circumscribed little villages in which they had passed all their years. Now they would learn to have dealings with people essentially different from themselves. Now they would collide with unaccustomed problems, learn to understand alien ways and alien languages, manage to survive in a grossly foreign environment.

Initially, they had to save up money for passage. Then they had to say good-bye to cherished relatives and friends, whom they could expect never to see again. They started their journey by traveling from their villages to the ports of embarkation. Some walked; the luckier trundled their few possessions into carts which they sold before boarding ship. Some paused along the road to work in the fields in order to eat. Before they even reached the ports of embarkation, they were subject to illness, accidents, storm and snow, even to attacks by outlaws.

After arriving at the ports, they often had to wait days, weeks, sometimes months, while they bargained with captains or agents for passage. Meanwhile, they crowded into cheap lodging houses near the quays, sleeping on straw in small, dark rooms, sometimes as many as forty in a room twelve by fifteen feet.

Until the middle of the nineteenth century the immigrants traveled in sailing vessels. The average trip from Liverpool to New York took forty days; but any estimate of time was hazardous, for the ship was subject to winds, tides, primitive navigation, unskilled seamanship and the whim of the captain. A good size for the tiny craft of those days was three hundred tons, and each one was crowded with anywhere from four hundred to a thousand passengers.

For the immigrants, their shipboard world was the steerage, that confined space below deck, usually about seventy-five feet long and twenty-five feet wide. In many vessels no one over five and a half feet tall could stand upright. Here they lived their days and nights, receiving their daily ration of vinegar-flavored water and trying to eke out sustenance from whatever provisions they had brought along. When their food ran out, they were often at the mercy of extortionate captains.

They huddled in their hard, cramped bunks, freezing when the hatches were open, stifling when they were closed. The only light came from a dim, swaying lantern. Night and day were indistinguishable. But they were ever aware of the treacherous winds and waves, the scampering of rats and the splash of burials. Diseases—cholera, yellow fever, smallpox and dysentery—took their toll. One in ten failed to survive the crossing.

Eventually the journey came to an end. The travelers saw the coast of America with mixed feelings of relief, excitement, trepidation and anxiety. For now, uprooted from old patterns of life, they found themselves, in Handlin's phrase, "in a prolonged state of crisis—crisis in the sense that they were, and remained, unsettled." They reached the new land exhausted by lack of rest, bad food, confinement and the strain of adjustment to new conditions. But they could not pause to recover their strength. They had no reserves of food or money; they had to keep moving until they found work. This meant new strains at a time when their capacity to cope with new problems had already been overburdened.

There were probably as many reasons for coming to America as there were people who came. It was a highly individual decision. Yet it can be said that three large forces—religious persecution, political oppression and economic hardship—provided the chief motives for the mass migrations to our shores. They were responding, in their own way, to the pledge of the Declaration of Independence: the promise of "life, liberty and the pursuit of happiness."

The search for freedom of worship has brought people to America from the days of the Pilgrims to modern times. In our own day, for example, anti-Semitic and anti-Christian persecution in Hitler's Germany and the Communist empire have driven people from their homes to seek refuge in America. Not all found what they sought immediately. The Puritans of the Massachusetts Bay Colony, who drove Roger Williams and Anne Hutchinson into the wilderness, showed as little tolerance for dissenting beliefs as the Anglicans of England had shown to them. Minority religious sects, from the Quakers and Shakers through the Catholics and Jews to the Mormons and Jehovah's Witnesses, have at various times suffered both discrimination and hostility in the United States.

But the very diversity of religious belief has made for religious toleration. In demanding freedom for itself, each sect had increasingly to permit freedom for others. The insistence of each successive wave of immigrants upon its right to practice its religion helped make freedom of worship a central part of the American creed. People who gambled their lives on the right to believe in their own God would not lightly surrender that right in a new society.

The second great force behind immigration has been political oppression. America has always been a refuge from tyranny. As a nation conceived in liberty, it has held out to the world the promise of respect for the rights of man. Every time a revolution has failed in Europe, every time a nation has succumbed to tyranny, men and women who love freedom have assembled their families and their belongings and set sail across the seas. Nor has this process come to an end in our own day. The Russian Revolution, the terrors of Hitler's Germany and Mussolini's Italy, the Communist suppression of the Hungarian Revolution of 1956, and the cruel measures of the Castro regime in Cuba—all have brought new thousands seeking sanctuary in the United States.

The economic factor has been more complex than the religious and political factors. From the very beginning, some have come to America in search of riches, some in flight from poverty and some because they were bought and sold and had no choice.

And the various reasons have intertwined. Thus some early arrivals were lured to these shores by dreams of amassing great wealth, like the Spanish conquistadors in Mexico and Peru. These adventurers, expecting quick profits in gold, soon found that real wealth lay in such crops as tobacco and cotton. As they built up the plantation economy in states like Virginia and the Carolinas, they needed cheap labor. So they began to import indentured servants from England, men and women who agreed to labor a term of years in exchange for eventual freedom, and slaves from Africa.

The process of industrialization in America increased the demand for cheap labor, and chaotic economic conditions in Europe increased the supply. If some immigrants continued to believe that the streets of New York were paved with gold, more were driven by the hunger and hardship of their native lands. The Irish Potato Famine of 1845 brought almost a million people to America in five years. American manufacturers advertised in European newspapers, offering to pay the passage of any man willing to come to America to work for them.

The immigrants who came for economic reasons contributed to the strength of the new society in several ways. Those who came from countries with advanced political and economic institutions brought with them faith in those institutions and experience in making them work. They also brought technical and managerial skills which contributed greatly to economic growth in the new land. Above all, they helped give America the extraordinary social mobility which is the essence of an open society.

In the community he had left, the immigrant usually had a fixed place. He would carry on his father's craft or trade; he would farm his father's land, or that small portion of it that was left to him after it was divided with his brothers. Only with the most exceptional talent and enterprise could he break out of the mold in which life had cast him. There was no such mold for him in the New World. Once having broken with the past, except for sentimental ties and cultural inheritance, he had to rely on his own abilities. It was the future and not the past to which he was compelled to address himself. Except for the Negro slave, he could go anywhere and do anything his talents permitted. A sprawling continent lay before him, and he had only to weld it together by canals, by railroads and by roads. If he failed to achieve the dream for himself, he could still retain it for his children.

This has been the foundation of American inventiveness and ingenuity, of the multiplicity of new enterprises, and of the success in achieving the highest standard of living anywhere in the world.

These were the major forces that triggered this massive migration. Every immigrant served to reinforce and strengthen those elements in American society that had attracted him in the first place. The motives of some were commonplace. The motives of others were noble. Taken together they add up to the strengths and weaknesses of America.

The wisest Americans have always understood the significance of the immigrant. Among the "long train of abuses and usurpations" that impelled the framers of the Declaration of Independence to the fateful step of separation was the charge that the British monarch had restricted immigration: "He has endeavoured to prevent the population of these States; for that reason obstructing the Laws for the Naturalization of Foreigners; refusing to pass others to encourage their migrations hither, and raising the conditions of new Appropriations of Lands."

CHAPTER 3

WAVES OF IMMIGRATION—THE PRE-REVOLUTIONARY FORCES

IMMIGRATION FLOWED TOWARD AMERICA IN A SERIES of continuous waves. Every new migration gathered force, built momentum, reached a crest and then merged imperceptibly into the great tide of people already on our shores.

The name "America" was given to this continent by a German mapmaker, Martin Waldseemüller, to honor an Italian explorer, Amerigo Vespucci. The three ships which discovered America sailed under a Spanish flag, were commanded by an Italian sea captain, and included in their crews an Englishman, an Irishman, a Jew and a Negro.

Long before the colonies were settled, the Spanish and French explorers left evidences of their visits on great expanses of the American wilderness: the Spanish in a wide arc across the southern part of the country, from Florida, where they founded St. Augustine, our oldest city, in 1565, through Texas and New Mexico, to California; the French, up and down the Mississippi and Ohio River valleys. Spanish influence can be seen today in our architecture, in the old missions, in family names and place names such as Los Angeles, San Francisco and Sacramento; the French influence is apparent in many towns and cities still bearing the names of the original settlements, such as Cadillac, Champlain and La Salle.

The first wave of settlement came with the colonists at Jamestown in 1607 and at Plymouth in 1620. It was predominantly English in origin. The urge for greater economic opportunity, together with the desire for religious freedom, impelled these people to leave their homes. Of all the groups that have come to America, these settlers had the most difficult physical environment to master, but the easiest social adjustment to make. They fought a rugged land, and that was hard. But they built a society in their own image, and never knew the hostility of the old toward the new that succeeding groups would meet.

The English, the numerical majority of the first settlers, gave America the basic foundation of its institutions: our form of government, our common law, our language, our tradition of freedom of religious worship. Some of these concepts have been modified as the nation has grown, but the basic elements remain. Those who came later built upon these foundations. But America was settled by immigrants from many countries, with diverse national ethnic and social backgrounds.

There were both indentured servants and profit-seeking aristocrats from England. There were farmers, both propertied and bankrupt, from Ireland. There were discharged soldiers, soldiers of fortune, scholars and intellectuals from Germany. The colonies welcomed all men, regardless of their origin or birth, so long as they could contribute to the building of the country. The Dutch settled Nieuw Amsterdam and explored the Hudson River. The Swedes came to Delaware. Polish, German and Italian craftsmen were eagerly solicited to join the struggling Virginia colonists in Jamestown. The Germans and Swiss opened up the back country in Pennsylvania, New York, Virginia and the Carolinas. French Huguenots took root in New England, New York, South Carolina and Georgia. The Scots and the Irish were in the vanguard that advanced the frontier beyond the Alleghenies. When Britain conquered Nieuw Amsterdam in 1664, it offered citizenship to immigrants of eighteen different nationalities.

At one time it seemed the continent might ultimately divide into three language sections: English, Spanish and French. But the English victories over the French and the purchase of territories held by the French and Spanish resulted in the creation of an indivisible country, with the same language, customs and government. Yet each ethnic strain left its own imprint on the new land.

Thus the very name of our country, "The United States of America," was borrowed from "The United States of the Netherlands." Many "typical American" activities are Dutch in origin. The immigrants from Holland brought to this country ice-skating, bowling, many forms of boating and golf (which they called *kolf*); they gave us waffles, cookies and that staple of the American menu, the doughnut (originally *kruller*). To our folklore they contributed the figure of Santa Claus and his reindeer, and the many tales of the Hudson Valley. Examples of their architecture can still be seen on the banks of the Hudson today.

French colonial immigration had two main sources. The

Protestant Huguenots came here in considerable numbers after persecution resumed as the result of the revocation of the
Edict of Nantes in 1685. The Catholic "Acadians" came here
after their exile from Nova Scotia in 1755 when that land fell
under British rule.

The Huguenots settled in the larger trading towns of
New England, later spreading down through Pennsylvania
and Virginia, and in South Carolina. A Huguenot family
presented Faneuil Hall, a shrine of American liberty, to the
city of Boston. Many of the beautiful houses which make
Charleston so picturesque today were built originally by Huguenots.

The Acadians, relatively few in numbers, scattered mostly
along the Eastern seaboard. But a colony of them settled in
Louisiana, along the bayous to the west and north of New
Orleans. They were relatively isolated, and as they grew in
number, they kept their language, their customs, their faith
and folklore, even abiding by the Napoleonic Code rather
than English law. Today, sometimes known as "Cajuns," they
provide one of the most distinctive ethnic elements on the
American scene.

During and after the French Revolution of 1789, French
musicians, dancing masters, tutors and wigmakers, once em-
ployed by the now deposed aristocrats, added a touch of grace
to the homespun life of the new nation. They introduced the
French art of cooking, as well as the cotillion, the waltz and
the quadrille. French-Spanish émigrés from the West Indies
made New Orleans into a great cultural and social center. The
first opera to be given in America was produced in that city.
The only major American city built according to a systematic

plan, Washington, D.C., was designed by the French Army engineer Major Pierre Charles L'Enfant.

The early Swedes, too, made their contribution to American culture—in particular, the knowledge of how to build houses from squared-off timbers. This structure was later to become the mark of the frontier, where it was known as the log cabin.

Over two thousand Jews came to this country in pre-Revolutionary days. Most were from Spain or Portugal. Some established themselves in the Dutch colony of Nieuw Amsterdam, after winning recognition of their right to trade, travel and live in the colony from Peter Stuyvesant. Others settled in Newport, Rhode Island, then a thriving center of the maritime trade. Many prospered as merchants in the West India trade, which included sugar, rum and molasses. The oldest synagogue in the United States, built in 1763, is located in Newport, Rhode Island.

Among the earliest settlers in Pennsylvania were Welsh farmers who came here for economic reasons and out of a desire to revive Welsh nationalism. In the years 1683–99, they were augmented by Welsh Quakers who came to escape religious persecution. Their presence is reflected by such place names as Bryn Mawr and Radnor, and in the sturdy farmhouses of the area, still standing after almost three hundred years.

The pre-Revolutionary Irish immigration is usually referred to as Scotch-Irish, since it consisted largely of Scots who had settled in Ireland during the seventeenth century.

These were the frontiersmen, ideally suited by their previous environment and experience to spearhead the drive against the colonial frontiers. They pushed out almost at once to the edge of the wilderness in Pennsylvania, Maryland and Maine, and down the Great Valley to the Carolina Piedmont. Through them, Presbyterianism became a powerful force on the frontier. The Scotch Presbyterians founded many institutions of higher learning, beginning with Princeton in 1746.

In 1683 thirteen German families arrived in Philadelphia. They were the forerunners of a substantial migration from Germany. With them there also came Swiss, Alsatians, Dutch and Bohemians. By the eve of the Revolution there were over 100,000 German immigrants and descendants of German immigrants living in the United States. They constituted the first numerical challenge to the hitherto predominantly English population.

Some were Pietists, Moravians and Mennonites, sects in some ways similar to the Quakers. They found in William Penn's colony a sympathetic climate in which they could practice their beliefs without interference.

Those of their descendants who live today in and around Lancaster County, Pennsylvania, are known as the "Pennsylvania Dutch." They have made of their land a model of conservationist farming. Nearly three hundred years after they first broke ground, their land is as fertile and productive as they found it. They built the first Conestoga wagon, a vehicle which was to prove immensely useful to the settlement of the West.

Other German immigrants were members of other religious groups, such as the Amish and the Dunkards, who like to be known as "the plain people." They have changed little in their folkways and religious practices. They still wear their traditional clothing and follow traditional customs, providing, like the Cajuns, a picturesque addition to the American scene.

Although there was no large-scale Italian immigration before the Revolution, there were many Italians prominent in American life. As early as 1610, craftsmen were brought from Italy by the colony of Virginia to start a glass trade. Later, others came and planted vineyards. Georgia invited them to organize a silk industry.

In all the large cities there were Italian doctors, merchants, innkeepers and teachers. They wandered everywhere as traveling musicians, held concerts and established music schools. Our first sculptors and our first interior decorators were Italian.

Although predominantly Catholic, the Italians had their own counterpart of the Puritans, the Waldensians. They were an independent sect from the Piedmont, in the north of Italy, who were invited by the Dutch colonial government to form settlements here. Some 167 of them accepted, and in 1657 they were brought to the New World to settle a tract of land set aside for them by the Nieuw Amsterdam government.

Poles, too, were present in pre-Revolutionary America. Originally, they, too, came at the invitation of the Dutch. Most of them were farmers, but some settled in what is now New York City, where one of them, Dr. Alexander Kurcyusz (Curtius), a prominent physician, founded the first Latin school. Pre-Revolutionary America also included Greeks, Russians and other Slavs, immigrants from Southeastern and Eastern Europe.

During the Revolutionary War itself, men came from

many other lands to help the new nation. Two Poles helped turn the tide toward victory. Thaddeus Kosciusko, a young engineer, offered his services early. He became an aide to General Washington and a major general in the engineers. His plans are credited with winning the Battle of Saratoga, a turning point in the war. Count Casimir Pulaski rose to the rank of general, fought heroically at Brandywine, Trenton and in other decisive engagements. He organized his own Polish Legion, ultimately giving his life to the new nation when he died as a result of a wound received at the Battle of Savannah. A German, Baron Friedrich Wilhelm von Steuben, did more than anyone else to shape the raw recruits into a disciplined army. A Frenchman, Marquis de Lafayette, has become something of an American folk hero for his part in the Revolution. He took a leading part in the campaign that led to the defeat of Cornwallis at Yorktown. The service of another Frenchman, Count de Rochambeau, who recruited over four thousand French volunteers, was almost as great.

Between a third and a half of the fighting men of the Revolutionary Army were of Scottish or Scotch-Irish descent. Many of those at Valley Forge were German.

A Pole of Portuguese-Jewish origin, Haym Salomon, risked his life to gain vital intelligence for the American cause. A Scotch-Irish immigrant, Robert Morris, helped finance the war.

Four signers of the Declaration of Independence were immigrants of Irish birth: Matthew Thornton, James Smith, George Taylor and Edward Rutledge. The great doctrine, "All men are created equal," incorporated in the Declaration by Thomas Jefferson, was paraphrased from the writing of Philip

Mazzei, an Italian-born patriot and pamphleteer, who was a close friend of Jefferson. Mazzei compiled the first accurate history of the colonies, which he wrote in French so that the European nations would be able to appreciate the political, social and economic conditions that characterized the new world.

A gravestone in the Shenandoah Valley of Virginia reads: "Here lies the remains of John Lewis, who slew the Irish lord, settled in Augusta County, located the town of Staunton and furnished five sons to fight the battles of the American Revolution." Statements like this not only speak eloquently of the contribution of one Irish family, but represent the sacrifices of many immigrants to this country even before it had won its independence.

CHAPTER 4

WAVES OF IMMIGRATION—THE POST-REVOLUTIONARY FORCES

AMERICAN INDEPENDENCE, THE SPREADING WESTWARD of the new nation, the beginnings of economic diversification and industrialization, all these factors gave immigration in the nineteenth century a new context and a new role. The gates were now flung open, and men and women in search of a new life came to these shores in ever-increasing numbers—150,000 in the 1820's, 1.7 million in the 1840's, 2.8 million in the 1870's, 5.2 million in the 1880's, 8.8 million in the first decade of the twentieth century. And, as the numbers increased, the sources changed. As the English had predominated in the seventeenth and eighteenth centuries, so the Irish and Germans predominated in the first half of the nineteenth and the Italians and East Europeans in the last part of the nineteenth and the early part of the twentieth centuries. Each new wave of immigration helped meet the needs of American development and made its distinctive contribution to the American character.

THE IRISH

The Irish were in the vanguard of the great waves of immigration to arrive during the nineteenth century. By 1850, after the potato famine, they had replaced England as the chief source of new settlers, making up 44 percent of the foreign-born in the United States. In the century between 1820 and 1920, some four and a quarter million people left Ireland to come to the United States.

They were mostly country folk, small farmers, cottagers and farm laborers. Yet they congregated mainly in cities along the Eastern seaboard, for they did not have the money to travel after reaching shore. Few could read or write; some spoke only Gaelic.

The Irish were the first to endure the scorn and discrimination later to be inflicted, to some degree at least, on each successive wave of immigrants by already settled "Americans." In speech and dress they seemed foreign; they were poor and unskilled; and they were arriving in overwhelming numbers. The Irish are perhaps the only people in our history with the distinction of having a political party, the Know-Nothings, formed against them. Their religion was later also the target of the American Protective Association and, in this century, the Ku Klux Klan.

The Irish found many doors closed to them, both socially and economically. Advertisements for jobs specified: "No Irish need apply." But there was manual labor to be done, and the Irish were ready to do it. They went to work as longshoremen, as ditch-diggers or as construction workers. When their

NOVA BRITANNIA.

OFFERING MOST,

Excellent fruites by Planting in
VIRGINIA.

Exciting all fuch as be well affected
to further the fame.

LONDON
Printed for SAMVEL MACHAM, and are to befold at
his Shop in Pauls Church-yard, at the
Signe of the Bul-head.
1 6 0 9.

The first Americans—members of scattered tribes—were native-born. All others were immigrants. Some came early, some later. After the centuries of exploration, when men came to discover and conquer but did not stay to settle, the first community in what is now the Continental United States was founded by the Spanish in St. Augustine, Florida, in 1565. Sir Walter Raleigh built a colony farther up the Atlantic coast in 1585 and called it Virginia; another colony at Roanoke was lost and its fate is still a mystery. In 1606, King James I of England granted charters for new settlements in Virginia. The illustration here is the title page of a leaflet printed in London in 1609 for the Council of Virginia to persuade Englishmen to emigrate. In the years to come many such leaflets, handbills and advertisements, steamship posters, and letters from colonists carried the good news of a land of freedom and opportunity.

Many of the first immigrants, like many of the most recent, came to America to escape oppression at home. Religious persecution led thousands to the New World—the Puritans to Massachusetts, Quakers to Pennsylvania and Delaware, French Huguenots to South Carolina. Above is a depiction from a contemporary document of the burning of religious books in Salzburg, part of the religious persecution that drove Lutherans to America. Some came to Georgia in 1732. Below, a contemporary drawing shows James Nailor, a Quaker, who, because of his religious belief, was whipped in 1656 by the hangman in London, his tongue bored through with a hot iron and his forehead branded. Such men came to America in search of freedom to worship God as their conscience directed.

Iames Nailor Quaker ſet 2 howers on the Pillory at Weſtminſter whiped by the Hang
man to the old Exchainge London, Som dayes after, Stood too howers more on the Pillory
.ͯ at the Exchainge, and there had his Tongue Bored throug with a hot Iron, &
Stigmatized in the Forehead with the Letter:B; Decem.ͬ 17 anno Domiı656ı

TO BE SOLD, on **board**
the *George-Town* Galley, *Thomas*
Crofthwaite Mafter, lying at *Frank-*
land's Wharff, fundry *Englifb*
SERVANTS, Men and Women,
well recommended, amongft whom are **Tradef-**
men, Hufbandmen, &c. indented for *Four Tears.*

Many of the first settlers did not come as
free men. Thousands, unemployed and
homeless, signed away their freedom for
a few years in exchange for transportation, coming as indentured servants to
work without wages. Redemptioners
agreed to be sold in America for the sum
of their passage. Above, an advertisement
for "English servants, Men and Women,
well recommended . . . indent[ur]ed for
Four Years."

At right is the deck plan of an eight-
eenth-century British slave ship. The first
African slaves were brought in 1619 to
Virginia. All such traffic in human lives
was outlawed by vote of Congress in
1807, although many slaves were brought
in illegally thereafter. Not until the
Emancipation Proclamation in 1863, the
war between North and South, and the
ratification of the Thirteenth Amendment
in 1865 were the slaves finally free. It
took another century for freedom to be
transformed into the beginning of first-
class citizenship.

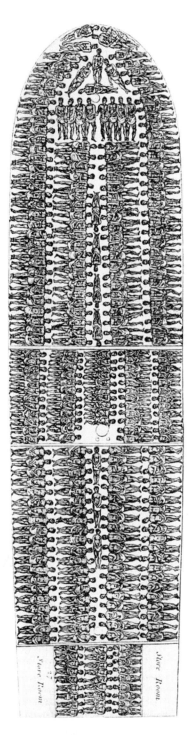

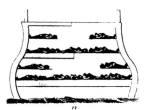

In the first half of the nineteenth century, immigration soared. Between 1815 and 1860, five million came. The largest number sailed from Ireland, victimized by starvation and typhus that followed the potato famine of 1845–1849. Crops failed, too, in Germany and in Holland, and many thousands, driven from the land, emigrated to the United States. Desperate families sold their last possessions for transportation, and in many cases landowners provided funds, wishing to free themselves of responsibility for a pauper class. Conditions on the crowded ships were often brutal, and a high percentage died before they reached the land of new hope. Above is a contemporary illustration of Irish famine victims.

Driven by economic need and the defeat of democracy in the revolutions of
1830 and 1848, well over a million Germans came in the fifteen years before
1860. Many were students and intellectuals, among them the social reformer
Carl Schurz. Political refugees came also from other lands. Bohemian na-
tionalists joined the Germans. Poles fled after the failure of revolts against
alien rule of their country. Hungarians, defeated in their struggle for freedom in 1848, sought a new life in America. Above is a contemporary illustration of fighting between the Prussian army and revolutionists at the barri-
cades in Frankfurt.

"Native Americans," native in the sense that their families had arrived in America earlier than some others, provoked anti-foreign riots in the 1840's. Men were killed and Catholic churches burned by mobs. About 1850 "Native Americans" formed a secret society, the Order of the Star-Spangled Banner. Members were instructed to answer "I know nothing" when questioned about their activities and consequently were labeled "Know-Nothings." For a few years they were a political power, electing governors in a number of states. Differences among them over the slavery issue led to a rapid decline of their influence in the years just before the Civil War. Above is a lithograph of a Philadelphia mob, in tall beaver hats, attacking the state militia in an anti-Catholic riot.

From 1870 to the end of the century, more than eleven million persons came to America, an increasing number from southern and eastern Europe and the Near East. The Burlingame Treaty with China in 1868 permitted Chinese immigration, and several thousand came, most to settle in California. But as American workers began to fear for their jobs, and as the depression of 1873 caused widespread unemployment, mobs fought the Chinese, killing some and burning the homes of others. The scene on the opposite page shows an anti-Chinese riot in Denver. The Chinese Exclusion Act of 1882 prohibited the immigration of Chinese laborers and denied American citizenship to native Chinese, a discriminatory act that remained in effect until World War II.

American immigrants gave their strength and skills to build a new country. Among the pioneers who moved West in the covered wagons to the open frontier were thousands of men and women who had just arrived in America. Inexpensive land lured many farmers to the Midwest. The Western railroads, built with the help of subsidies and land grants from the government, sold the land to get funds to build the roads. They sent agents to Europe to hunt for prospective immigrants, and advertised widely overseas. Upper right, an advertisement of the Illinois Central describing farms of $8 to $12 an acre available with long credit in Illinois, "the Garden State of America." Lower right, a pioneer's sod home on the Nebraska prairie, South Loup, Custer County, 1892.

THE FINEST FARMING LANDS

WHEAT — CORN — COTTON — FRUITS & VEGETABLES

EQUAL TO ANY IN THE WORLD!!!

MAY BE PROCURED

At FROM $8 to $12 PER ACRE.

Near Markets, Schools, Railroads, Churches, and all the blessings of Civilization.

1,200,000 Acres, in Farms of 40, 80, 120, 160 Acres and upwards, in
ILLINOIS, the Garden State of America.

Immigrants helped America make the transition to an industrial society. Chinese and Irish railroad gangs, recruited to meet the urgent labor demands, laid tracks that brought the East and West together in 1869—the Chinese from the West on the Central Pacific, the Irish from the East on the Union Pacific. Here, a photograph of the construction of the St. Paul, Minneapolis and Manitoba Railroad in 1887.

Immigrants—many from Scandinavia—were recruited for the lumber crews that felled timber in the Great Northwest. Here a crew poses for its portrait in 1906.

The great coal and steel industries owed much to the immigrant groups, among them the Welsh and Poles who came to Pennsylvania and Ohio in the nineteenth century. Here, a scene in an anthracite mine.

The New Colossus.

Not like the brazen giant of Greek fame,
With conquering limbs astride from land to land;
Here at our sea-washed, sunset-gates shall stand
A mighty woman with a torch, whose flame
Is the imprisoned lightning, and her name
Mother of Exiles. From her beacon-hand
Glows world-wide welcome, her mild eyes command
The air-bridged harbor that twin-cities frame.

"Keep, ancient lands, your storied pomp!" cries she
With silent lips. "Give me your tired, your poor,
Your huddled masses yearning to breathe free,
The wretched refuse of your teeming shore,
Send these, the homeless, tempest-tost to me,
I lift my lamp beside the golden door!"

Emma Lazarus,

November 2nd 1883.

The Statue of Liberty in New York Harbor has symbolized freedom for generations of immigrants. Mounted on its pedestal is a tablet reproducing a poem, "The New Colossus." It was written in 1883 by Emma Lazarus, who was born in New York of Jewish parentage and who was deeply concerned with the plight of Jews driven from Russia to the United States. The original manuscript of her famous poem is reproduced above.

Future Americans crowded every available steamship. Here and on the opposite page are typical scenes on the decks of Atlantic liners in the first years of the twentieth century.

An Italian immigrant family stands on the deck of a ferry boat plying between Ellis Island, first stop for European immigrants, and New York City. Between 1820 and 1963, more than five million Italians came to America.

An Italian family with their bundled belongings, waiting for instructions. Many such families took jobs in heavy industry or on the railroad. Others settled in the urban centers of the East.

Persons of all races, all nations, and all conditions of life sought refuge in America.

At Ellis Island, immigrants in the early 1900's anxiously wait to learn whether they will be permitted to enter the Promised Land of America.

Immigrants at Ellis Island answered questions, submitted to physical and psychological examinations, and then (if admitted) were ready to be transported to their destinations. Some unfortunate ones were rejected. Steamship companies, by an act of Congress in 1891, were compelled to carry back to Europe all passengers rejected by United States inspectors. Above, women immigrants at a medical examination on Ellis Island around 1910. On the opposite page, above, an inspector gives an intelligence test; below, immigrants are handed tags listing assignments to railroad cars for transportation to their next destination.

German

Armenian

The strong, dynamic faces of new Americans from eight countries, typical

Danish

Czech

Laplander

Polish

of those who came from many lands and from all of the inhabited continents:

Chinese

Albanian

Many immigrants got no farther than their first stop, New York City. Thousands settled in the Lower East Side, living in crowded tenements, as here (above) at Hester and Clinton streets.

(Opposite page) Sweatshops were organized in tenement homes and lofts during the first years of the twentieth century. Even children were pressed into work as families struggled to survive.

The hooded legions of the Ku Klux Klan brought terror to American Negroes, Catholics, Jews, and to almost all immigrant groups. The night riders used whips and guns and the lynching rope to spread their gospel of hate. Here, a photograph of a Klan rally reproduced from a Klan magazine of the 1920's.

The Pledge of Allegiance to the American flag at a citizenship class in 1940.

Symbol of the Nazi cancer that was to consume much of Europe is the above photograph of book burning by Nazi students in 1933. Thousands of books were destroyed by young fanatics. With the rise of Hitler and virulent anti-Semitism in the 1930's, millions of Jews tried desperately to escape from Germany and Nazi-occupied countries. Many nations of Europe, as well as the United States, were reluctant to admit the despairing multitudes. Before the end, six million Jews had died in concentration camps and gas chambers. But some escaped from the Nazis. Below, Albert Einstein, one of the greatest scientists in history, takes the Oath of Allegiance to the United States, with his daughter, Margot (right), in Trenton, New Jersey.

"What Happened To The One We Used To Have?"

U.S. IMMIGRATION POLICY

From *The Herblock Book* (Beacon Press, 1952)

Restrictive immigration policy, stimulated in the 1920's by fear of competition from foreign labor and by the onset of isolationism, continued down to and through World War II. While thousands waited in despair for the Golden Door to open, Americans debated. Here, an eloquent 1946 cartoon by Herblock denouncing the lack of compassion of Americans who had forgotten their history and their own origins.

Refugees from Europe, victims of Nazi persecution and of war, came to America when the gates were opened. In 1948 Congress passed the Displaced Persons Act to admit more than 400,000. Above, the arrival of DP's in the early 1950's; opposite page, a reunion on the docks of New York, around 1947.

Political persecution was not ended by the destruction of Nazism or by the victory of World War II. Hundreds of thousands were made homeless in the 1950's by Communist oppression behind the Iron Curtain. In 1953 Congress passed the Refugee Relief Act to admit around 200,000 refugees, and this act made it possible for approximately 30,000 freedom fighters who escaped from Hungary after the 1956 anti-Soviet revolution to be admitted to the United States. Here a family crosses the icy marshland at Andau, Austria, in November, 1956, on their flight to freedom. During those weeks more than a thousand a day escaped through Andau.

earnings were not enough to support their families, their wives and daughters obtained employment as servants.

Contractors usually met them at the dock. The Erie Canal, linking New York with the Great Lakes in 1825, and other canals in Massachusetts, New Jersey, Pennsylvania and Maryland were largely built by Irish labor. But the canals soon became obsolete, and the frenzied building of railroads followed. In the three decades from 1830 to 1860, a network of thirty thousand miles of rails was laid across the middle part of the country. Again Irish labor furnished the muscle. When railroad construction was pushed westward in the latter part of the century, the Irish again figured prominently, by now often as foremen and section bosses. They also provided, at the same time, a supply of cheap labor for the mills of Rhode Island and Massachusetts and the coal mines of Pennsylvania.

But as the years passed and new generations were born, things began to change. Gradually, rung by rung, the Irish climbed up the economic and social ladder. Some settled on farms, especially along the canals they had dug. But it was in the cities that they found their principal outlet, in areas in which they could demonstrate their abilities of self-expression, of administration and organization. They gravitated first into law and from that into politics and government. Having experienced for themselves the handicaps of illiteracy, they were determined that their children would have the advantages of education. To that end, they not only started parochial schools, but founded such institutions of higher learning as Notre Dame, Fordham, Holy Cross, Villanova, St. Louis University, Catholic University and Georgetown. They became teachers, writers, journalists, labor organizers, orators and priests. As an expanding society offered more opportunities, they swelled not only the civil service rosters, but the ranks of clerical and administrative workers in industry.

The Irish eased the way for other immigrant groups and speeded their assimilation in several ways. They firmly established the Catholic Church, originally French on this continent, as an English-speaking institution. The schools they founded offered educational opportunities to children of later immigrants of other tongues. The Irish had their own press, their own fraternal orders and their own charitable organizations.

Irish labor leaders fought for the rights of other groups as well as their own. Workers of Irish descent helped organize the Knights of Labor, the first big national union, which was a forerunner of the American Federation of Labor.

THE GERMANS

Between 1830 and 1930, the period of the greatest migration from Europe to the United States, Germany sent six million people to the United States—more than any other nation. Their migrations, increasing in numbers after 1850, overlapped the Irish, whose immigration declined.

The Germans were unique among immigrant groups in their wide dispersal, both geographically and occupationally. This was due, at least in part, to the fact that most of them came with some resources, and were not forced to cluster along the Eastern seaboard. Attracted to the United States by cheap public and railroad lands, and later by free homesteads, the German farmer helped to farm the New West and to cultivate the Mississippi Valley. German artisans, much sought after because of their skills, became an important factor in industrial expansion.

Almost every state in the Union profited from their intellectual and material contributions. Hard-working and knowledgeable about agricultural methods, the Germans became propagators of scientific farming, crop rotation, soil conservation. They share with the Scandinavians the credit for turning millions of acres of wilderness into productive farm land.

The urban settlers lent a distinctive German flavor to many of our cities. Cincinnati, then known as "Queen City" of the West, Baltimore, St. Louis, Minneapolis and Milwaukee, all had substantial German populations. Milwaukee has perhaps retained its distinctive German character longer than any of the others.

In these urban centers Germans entered the fields of education, science, engineering and the arts. German immigrants founded and developed industrial enterprises in the fields of lumbering, food-processing, brewing, steel-making, electrical engineering, piano-making, railroading and printing.

A small but significant part of the German immigration consisted of political refugees. Reaction in Germany against the reform ideas of the French Revolution had caused heavy suppression of liberal thought. There was strict censorship of the press, of public meetings and of the schools and universities. Nevertheless, a liberal movement had emerged, nurtured in the universities by young intellectuals. This movement led to unsuccessful revolutions in 1830 and 1848. The United States welcomed a large number of veterans of 1848—men of education, substance and social standing, like Carl Schurz, the statesman and reformer, and General Franz Sigel. In addition, some of the German religious groups established utopian communities in parts of Pennsylvania, Ohio, Indiana, Texas and Oregon.

German immigration reflected all the chaotic conditions of Central Europe after Napoleon: the population growth, the widespread hunger, the religious dissension and oppression. The Germans included Lutherans, Jews and Catholics, as well as freethinkers. Their talents, training and background greatly enriched the burgeoning nation.

To the influence of the German immigrants in particular—although all minority groups contributed—we owe the mellowing of the austere Puritan imprint on our daily lives. The Puritans observed the Sabbath as a day of silence and solemnity. The Germans clung to their concept of the "Continental Sunday" as a day, not only of churchgoing, but also of relaxation, of picnics, of visiting, of quiet drinking in beer gardens while listening to the music of a band.

The Christmas ritual of religious services combined with exchanging gifts around the Christmas tree is of German origin. So, too, is the celebration of the New Year.

The fact that today almost every large American city has its symphony orchestra can be traced to the influence of the German migration. Leopold Damrosch and his son, Walter, helped build the famous New York Philharmonic. Originally composed mainly of German immigrant musicians and called the Germania Orchestra, it became the seed bed of similar organizations all over the country. This tradition was carried to the Midwest by Frederick Stock and to Boston by Carl Zerrahn. Others spread this form of cultural expression to additional urban centers throughout the land.

Community singing and glee clubs owe much to the German immigrant, who remembered his singing societies. The first *Männerchor* was founded in Philadelphia in 1835; the first *Liederkranz* was organized in Baltimore in 1836. Their counterparts have been a feature of the German-American community everywhere.

The ideas of German immigrants helped to shape our educational system. They introduced the kindergarten, or "children's play school." They also promoted the concept of the state-endowed university, patterned after the German university. The University of Michigan, founded in 1837, was the first such school to add to the philosophy of general liberal arts education an emphasis upon vocational training. The colonial concept of a university as a place to prepare gentlemen for a life of leisured culture was modified to include training in specialized skills.

The program of physical education in the schools had its roots in the *Turnverein,* or German gymnastic society. It was adopted and introduced to the American public by the YMCA.

German immigrant influence has been pervasive, in our language, in our mores, in our customs and in our basic philosophy. Even the hamburger, the frankfurter and the delicatessen, that omnipresent neighborhood institution, came to us via the German immigrants.

Although they were mostly Democrats prior to 1850,

the Germans broke party lines in the decade before the Civil War and played a prominent part in the formation of the Republican party. They were most united on two issues. They opposed the Blue Laws, and they vigorously fought the extension of slavery into new territories. Indeed, the first protest against Negro slavery came from Germantown settlers, led by Franz Pastorius, in 1688.

During the Civil War they fought on both sides. Following the Civil War, Germans infused the faltering American labor movement with new strength by organizing craft unions for printers, watchmakers, carpenters, ironworkers, locksmiths, butchers and bakers.

Adjusting with relative ease, they did not feel the sting of ethnic discrimination until the outbreak of the First World War, when they became targets of wartime hysteria. This hysteria even caused overardent "patriots" to call sauerkraut "Liberty cabbage" and hamburger "Salisbury steak." Nonetheless, when the United States entered the war in 1917, men of German ancestry entered the armed forces of the United States and served with distinction.

As the Second World War drew near, Americans of German descent faced another test. Only a few joined the pro-Nazi German-American Bund, and many of those left as soon as they discovered its real nature. More "older Americans" than those of German descent could be counted in the ranks of America-Firsters. Again, after the U.S. was attacked, descendants of German immigrants fought with valor in our armed services.

THE SCANDINAVIANS

Scandinavian immigrants left their homelands for economic rather than political or religious reasons. In America they found a political and social climate wholly compatible with their prior experience. Democratic institutions and a homogeneous society were already developing in Scandinavia, in an atmosphere of comparative tranquillity.

The seemingly limitless availability of farm land in America was an attractive prospect to land-hungry people.

The tide of Scandinavian immigration overlapped the tide of German immigration just as the Germans overlapped the Irish. The Swedes came first. They started coming about 1840, reaching their crest after 1860. Between 1840 and 1930, about 1.3 million Swedes came to the United States. In the 1880's migrations of other Scandinavians—Danes, Finns, Icelanders and principally the Norwegians—also reached their peak.

Following the Erie Canal and the Great Lakes, the Swedes pushed westward until they found a familiar landscape in the prairie states of the upper Mississippi Valley. There they settled.

The first colony of these Swedes settled at a place they named Pine Lakes (now New Upsala), in Wisconsin, in 1841. Later colonists showed a preference for a broad belt of land extending westward from Michigan, through Illinois, Wisconsin, Minnesota, Nebraska, Iowa and Kansas.

Other Scandinavian migrations followed more or less the same geographical pattern, except for the Norwegians. Although not so large numerically as other immigrant groups,

Norwegian immigration in proportion to their population at home was second only to the Irish. Some of the Norwegians drove far west to the Dakotas, Oregon and Washington. Norwegian immigration to the United States is estimated at 840,000; Danes at 350,000. Most Scandinavians settled in rural areas, except for the Finns, some of whom went to work in the copper mines of Michigan or the iron mines of Minnesota.

Physically hardy, conditioned by the rigors of life at home to withstand the hardships of the frontier, the Scandinavians made ideal pioneers. Ole Rölvaag, the Norwegian-American novelist, movingly chronicled their struggles in *Giants in the Earth*.

Often they started their homesteading in sod huts, some of which were no more than holes in a hillside shored up with logs, with greased-paper windows. They looked forward to the day they could live in a log cabin or in a house. Then began the struggle with the unrelenting forces of nature: hailstorms, droughts, blizzards, plagues of grasshoppers and locusts. But they endured.

America was an expanding continent in urgent need of housing. It was the Swedes, familiar with the ax and the saw—called "the Swedish fiddle"—who went into the forests across the Northern United States, felled the logs, slid them into the streams and sent them on their way to the mills, where they were cut into boards to provide shelter for millions of other immigrants. Norwegians and Finns were also among the loggers. On the West Coast the Norwegians tended to become fishermen.

The Swedes did many other things too. In the long nights

of the Swedish winter, they had learned to fashion things with their hands and had become skilled craftsmen and artisans. The "do-it-yourself" hobbyist of today is an avocational descendant of the Swedes. Manual training in our own public school system is derived from a basic course in the Swedish schools.

The Scandinavians were avid supporters of the public school system. And they contributed to the school system and to education generally in a variety of ways. The home economics courses of our public schools were introduced by Scandinavians. They also helped launch adult education programs. The 4-H Clubs, now an international as well as a national institution, were originated at a farm school in Minnesota by Americans of Scandinavian descent. A number of colleges today stand as monuments to the early efforts of Norwegians and Swedes to make higher learning available. Among these are Augustana College in Illinois, Gustavus Adolphus in Minnesota, Bethany College in Kansas and Luther College in Nebraska. All were founded by Swedish immigrants. Luther College in Iowa and St. Olaf College in Minnesota were founded by the Norwegians. They have added to our cultural life with their choral groups and singing societies.

With their background, it was inevitable that the Swedes would develop many engineers, scientists and inventors. One of the most famous was John Ericsson, who not only designed the *Monitor*, one of the first armor-clad ships, but also perfected the screw propeller.

The Danes, who had an intimate knowledge of animal husbandry, laid the foundations of our dairy industry and early creamery cooperatives. Together with the Germans and the Swiss, they developed cheese-making into an American industry.

Since the Danes were primarily agriculturists, it is curious that the one who made the most distinctive individual contribution was a city boy, Jacob Riis. As a crusading journalist and documentary photographer, he exposed the conditions under which other immigrants lived and worked in New York, and was instrumental in bringing about major social reforms.

Politically, Scandinavians cannot be classified into a single mold. At times they have been conservative. At times they have provided support for such liberal movements as the Farmer-Labor party, Senator Robert M. La Follette's Progressive party and the Non-Partisan League. Both major parties have benefited from Scandinavian political thought, and both major parties have had Scandinavians in both state and federal office.

OTHER IMMIGRANT GROUPS

Toward the end of the nineteenth century, emigration to America underwent a significant change. Large numbers of Italians, Russians, Poles, Czechs, Hungarians, Rumanians, Bulgarians, Austrians and Greeks began to arrive. Their coming created new problems and gave rise to new tensions.

For these people the language barrier was even greater than it had been for earlier groups, and the gap between the world they had left behind and the one to which they came was wider. For the most part, these were people of the land

and, for the most part, too, they were forced to settle in the cities when they reached America. Most large cities had well-defined "Little Italys" or "Little Polands" by 1910. In the 1960 census, New York City had more people of Italian birth or parentage than did Rome.

The history of cities shows that when conditions become overcrowded, when people are poor and when living conditions are bad, tensions run high. This is a situation that feeds on itself; poverty and crime in one group breed fear and hostility in others. This, in turn, impedes the acceptance and progress of the first group, thus prolonging its depressed condition. This was the dismal situation that faced many of the Southern and Eastern European immigrants just as it had faced some of the earlier waves of immigrants. One New York newspaper had these intemperate words for the newly arrived Italians; "The flood gates are open. The bars are down. The sally-ports are unguarded. The dam is washed away. The sewer is choked . . . the scum of immigration is viscerating upon our shores. The horde of $9.60 steerage slime is being siphoned upon us from Continental mud tanks."

Italy has contributed more immigrants to the United States than any country except Germany. Over five million Italians came to this country between 1820 and 1963. Large-scale immigration began in 1880, and almost four million Italian immigrants arrived in the present century.

The first Italians were farmers and artisans from northern Italy. Some planted vineyards in Vineland, New Jersey, in the Finger Lakes region of New York State and in California, where they inaugurated our domestic wine industry. Others settled on the periphery of cities, where they started truck gardens.

But most Italians were peasants from the south. They
came because of neither religious persecution nor political re-
pression, but simply in search of a brighter future. Population
in Italy was straining the limits of the country's resources and
more and more people had to eke out a living from small plots
of land, held in many instances by oppressive landlords.

In many ways the experience of the later Italian immigrants parallels the story of the Irish. Mostly farmers, their
lack of financial resources kept them from reaching the rural
areas of the United States. Instead, they crowded into cities
along the Eastern seaboard, often segregating themselves by
province, even by village, in a density as high as four thousand to the city block.

Untrained in special skills and unfamiliar with the language, they had to rely on unskilled labor jobs to earn a
living. Italians thus filled the gap left by earlier immigrant
groups who had now moved up the economic ladder. As
bricklayers, masons, stonecutters, ditchdiggers and hod car-
riers, they helped build our cities, subways and skyscrapers.
They worked on the railroads and the dams, went into the
coal mines, iron mines and factories. Some found a place in
urban life as small storekeepers, peddlers, shoemakers, bar-
bers and tailors. Wages were small and families were large.
In the old country everyone worked. Here everyone worked
too. Wives went into the needle trades. Boys picked up what
pennies they could as news vendors, bootblacks and errand-
runners. Through these difficult years of poverty, toil and be-
wilderment, the Italians were bolstered by their adherence to
the church, the strength of their family ties, Italian-language
newspapers and their fraternal orders. But they overcame

obstacles of prejudice and misunderstanding quickly, and they have found places of importance in almost every phase of American life. Citizens of Italian descent are among our leading bankers, contractors, food importers, educators, labor leaders and government officials. Italians have made special contributions to the emergence of American culture, enriching our music, art and architecture.

An Italian, Filippo Traetta (Philip Trajetta), founded the American Conservatory in Boston in 1800, and another in Philadelphia shortly thereafter. Another Italian, Lorenzo da Ponte, brought the first Italian opera troupe to New York in 1832, where it developed into a permanent institution. Italians have founded and supported the opera as an institution in New York, Chicago, San Francisco and other large cities, providing from their ranks many impresarios and singers. Italian-born music teachers and bandmasters are numerous. Arturo Toscanini, for many years leader of the New York Philharmonic, and our most distinguished conductor of recent years, was Italian-born.

Italians have also been among our most prominent sculptors, architects and artists. A West Indian and a Frenchman designed our nation's Capitol. An Italian beautified it. Constantino Brumidi painted the historical frieze in the rotunda of the Capitol building. Other Italian painters and sculptors depicted our history in paintings, murals, friezes and statues. Historical monuments and statues up and down the country have been wrought by Italian-American sculptors. On a humbler scale, the taste and skill of Italian-American landscape gardeners and architects have placed our homes and communities in beautiful settings.

About the time the Italians began coming, other great tides of immigration from the countries of Eastern and Southeastern Europe also began arriving in the United States. In the years between 1820 and 1963 these areas, Italy included, sent over fifteen million immigrants to our shores.

They came for all manner of reasons: political upheavals, religious persecution, hopes for economic betterment. They comprised a wide ethnic variety, from Lithuanians and Latvians on the Baltic to Greeks, Turks and Armenians on the eastern Mediterranean. They brought with them a bewildering variety of language, dress, custom, ideology and religious belief. To many Americans already here who had grown accustomed to a common way of life, they presented a dismaying bedlam, difficult to understand and more difficult to respond to. Indeed, because of the many changes in national boundaries and prior migrations of races within that area of Europe, there is no way of accurately reporting on them statistically.

The largest number from any of these countries of Eastern Europe were Poles, who for 125 years had been under the domination of Russia, Germany and Austria-Hungary. Some followed the pattern of the Germans and Scandinavians, settling on individual farms or forming small rural communities which still bear Polish place names. But most gravitated to the cities. Four-fifths were Roman Catholic. Longer than most immigrant groups they kept their language, their customs and their dances. At first, like other immigrants, they lived under substandard conditions. Gradually they, too, improved their status. They aspired to own their own homes and their own plots of land. In Hamtramck, Michigan, an almost wholly Polish community, three-quarters of the residents own their own homes.

By 1963, almost 130,000 Czechs had migrated to this country. They tended to gravitate to the farming communities. It is one of these homesteads that is portrayed by novelist Willa Cather in *My Antonia.* They also formed enclaves in cities, principally in Chicago, Cleveland and New York.

A potent force in the development of Czech life in this country has been the *Sokol,* a traditional cultural, social and gymnastic society. These societies stressed high standards of physical fitness and an interest in singing, music and literature.

The immigrants from Old Russia are estimated at almost three and a half million. Most of this wave of immigration went into the mines and factories. However, there were also many Russian intellectuals, scientists, scholars, musicians, writers and artists, who came here usually during periods of political oppression.

Most students of the history of immigration to America make special mention of the Jews. Although they appeared as part of several of the waves of immigration, they warrant separate discussion because of their religion, culture and historical background.

In colonial times most Jews in America were of Spanish-Portuguese origin. Throughout the nineteenth century most came from Germany. Beginning at the end of the nineteenth century they began to come in large numbers from Russia, Poland, Austria-Hungary, Rumania and, in smaller numbers, from almost every European nation. The American Jewish population today numbers approximately six million.

The Jews who came during the early nineteenth century

were often peddlers, wandering throughout the land with their packs and their carts or settling down to open small stores. They prospered in this era of opportunity and expansion, for from these humble beginnings have grown many of our large department stores and mercantile establishments.

The exodus from Germany after 1848 brought Jewish intellectuals, philosophers, educators, political leaders and social reformers. These shared much the same experiences as the other immigrants. "Like the Scandinavian Lutherans and the Irish Catholics," says Oscar Handlin, "they appeared merely to maintain their distinctive heritage while sharing the rights and obligations of other Americans within a free society."

At the turn of the century the Jews fleeing persecution in Russia came in such numbers that they could not be so readily absorbed into the mainstream of life as the earlier comers. They clustered in Jewish communities within the large cities, like New York.

Like the Irish and the Italians before them, they had to work at whatever they could find. Most found an outlet for their skills in the needle trades, as garment workers, hatmakers and furriers. Often they worked in sweatshops. In an effort to improve working conditions (which involved child labor and other forms of exploitation), they joined with other immigrant workers to form, in 1900, the International Ladies' Garment Workers Union. In time, they developed the clothing industry as we know it today, centered in New York but reaching into every small town and rural area. The experience and tradition of these pioneers produced many effective leaders in the labor movement, such as Morris Hillquit, Sidney Hillman, Jacob Potofsky and David Dubinsky.

Jewish immigrants have also made immense contributions to thought: as scholars, as educators, as scientists, as judges and lawyers, as journalists, as literary figures. Refugee scientists such as Albert Einstein and Edward Teller brought great scientific knowledge to this country.

Immigration from the Orient in the latter part of the nineteenth century was confined chiefly to California and the West Coast. Our behavior toward these groups of newcomers represented a shameful episode in our relationships to those seeking the hospitality of our shores. They were often mobbed and stoned by native Americans. The Chinese suffered and were barred from our shores as far back as the Chinese Exclusion Act of 1882. After the Japanese attack on Pearl Harbor many Japanese-Americans were victimized by prejudice and unreasoning discrimination. They were arbitrarily shipped to relocation camps. It took the extraordinary battlefield accomplishments of the nisei, Americans of Japanese descent, fighting in the U.S. Army in Europe, to help restore our perspective. While our attitude toward these citizens has been greatly improved over the years, many inequities in the law regarding Oriental immigration must still be redressed.

Today many of our newcomers are from Mexico and Puerto Rico. We sometimes forget that Puerto Ricans are U.S. citizens by birth and therefore cannot be considered immigrants. Nonetheless, they often receive the same discriminatory treatment and opprobrium that were faced by other waves of newcomers. The same things are said today of Puerto Ricans and Mexicans that were once said of Irish, Italians, Germans and Jews: "They'll never adjust; they can't learn the language; they won't be absorbed."

Perhaps our brightest hope for the future lies in the lessons of the past. The people who have come to this country have made America, in the words of one perceptive writer, "a heterogeneous race but a homogeneous nation."

In sum, then, we can see that as each new wave of immigration has reached America it has been faced with problems, not only the problems that come with making new homes and learning new jobs, but, more important, the problems of getting along with people of different backgrounds and habits.

Each new group was met by the groups already in America, and adjustment was often difficult and painful. The early English settlers had to find ways to get along with the Indians; the Irish who followed were met by these "Yankees"; German immigrants faced both Yankee and Irish; and so it has gone down to the latest group of Hungarian refugees. Somehow, the difficult adjustments are made and people get down to the tasks of earning a living, raising a family, living with their new neighbors and, in the process, building a nation.

CHAPTER 5

THE IMMIGRANT CONTRIBUTION

OSCAR HANDLIN HAS SAID, "ONCE I THOUGHT TO write a history of the immigrants in America. Then I discovered that the immigrants *were* American history." In the same sense, we cannot really speak of a particular "immigrant contribution" to America because all Americans have been immigrants or the descendants of immigrants; even the Indians, as mentioned before, migrated to the American continent. We can only speak of people whose roots in America are older or newer. Yet each wave of immigration left its own imprint on American society; each made its distinctive "contribution" to the building of the nation and the evolution of American life. Indeed, if, as some of the older immigrants like to do, we were to restrict the definition of immigrants to the 42 million people who came to the United States *after* the Declaration of Independence, we would have to conclude that our history and our society would have been vastly different if they all had stayed at home.

As we have seen, people migrated to the United States for

a variety of reasons. But nearly all shared two great hopes: the hope for personal freedom and the hope for economic opportunity. In consequence, the impact of immigration has been broadly to confirm the impulses in American life demanding more political liberty and more economic growth.

So, of the fifty-six signers of the Declaration of Independence, eighteen were of non-English stock and eight were first-generation immigrants. Two immigrants—the West Indian Alexander Hamilton, who was Washington's Secretary of the Treasury, and the Swiss Albert Gallatin, who held the same office under Jefferson—established the financial policies of the young republic. A German farmer wrote home from Missouri in 1834,

> If you wish to see our whole family living in . . . a country where freedom of speech obtains, where no spies are eavesdropping, where no simpletons criticize your every word and seek to detect therein a venom that might endanger the life of the state, the church and the home, in short, if you wish to be really happy and independent, then come here.

Every ethnic minority, in seeking its own freedom, helped strengthen the fabric of liberty in American life.

Similarly, every aspect of the American economy has profited from the contributions of immigrants. We all know, of course, about the spectacular immigrant successes: the men who came from foreign lands, sought their fortunes in the United States and made striking contributions, industrial and scientific, not only to their chosen country but to the entire world. In 1953 the President's Commission on Immigration and Naturalization mentioned the following:

Industrialists: Andrew Carnegie (Scot), in the steel industry; John Jacob Astor (German), in the fur trade; Michael Cudahy (Irish), of the meat-packing industry; the Du Ponts (French), of the munitions and chemical industry; Charles L. Fleischmann (Hungarian), of the yeast business; David Sarnoff (Russian), of the radio industry; and William S. Knudsen (Danish), of the automobile industry.

Scientists and inventors: Among those whose genius has benefited the United States are Albert Einstein (German), in physics; Michael Pupin (Serbian), in electricity; Enrico Fermi (Italian), in atomic research; John Ericsson (Swedish), who invented the ironclad ship and the screw propeller; Giuseppe Bellanca (Italian) and Igor Sikorsky (Russian), who made outstanding contributions to airplane development; John A. Udden (Swedish), who was responsible for opening the Texas oil fields; Lucas P. Kyrides (Greek), industrial chemistry; David Thomas (Welsh), who invented the hot blast furnace; Alexander Graham Bell (Scot), who invented the telephone; Conrad Hubert (Russian), who invented the flashlight; and Ottmar Mergenthaler (German), who invented the linotype machine.

But the anonymous immigrant played his indispensable role too. Between 1880 and 1920 America became the industrial and agricultural giant of the world as well as the world's leading creditor nation. This could not have been done without the hard labor, the technical skills and the entrepreneurial ability of the 23.5 million people who came to America in this period.

Significant as the immigrant role was in politics and in the economy, the immigrant contribution to the professions and the arts was perhaps even greater. Charles O. Paullin's analysis of the *Dictionary of American Biography* shows that, of the eighteenth- and nineteenth-century figures, 20 percent of the businessmen, 20 percent of the scholars and scientists, 23 percent of the painters, 24 percent of the engineers, 28 percent of the architects, 29 percent of the clergymen, 46 percent of the musicians and 61 percent of the actors were of foreign birth—a remarkable measure of the impact of immigration on American culture. And not only have many American writers and artists themselves been immigrants or the children of immigrants, but immigration has provided American literature with one of its major themes.

Perhaps the most pervasive influence of immigration is to be found in the innumerable details of life and the customs and habits brought by millions of people who never became famous. This impact was felt from the bottom up, and these contributions to American institutions may be the ones which most intimately affect the lives of all Americans.

In the area of religion, all the major American faiths were brought to this country from abroad. The multiplicity of sects established the American tradition of religious pluralism and assured to all the freedom of worship and separation of church and state pledged in the Bill of Rights.

So, too, in the very way we speak, immigration has altered American life. In greatly enriching the American vocabulary, it has been a major force in establishing "the American language," which, as H. L. Mencken demonstrated thirty years ago, had diverged materially from the mother tongue as spoken in Britain. Even the American dinner table has felt the impact. One writer has suggested that "typical American menus" might include some of the following dishes: "Irish stew, chop suey, goulash, chile con carne, ravioli, knackwurst mit sauerkraut, Yorkshire pudding, Welsh rarebit, borsch, gefilte fish, Spanish omelet, caviar, mayonnaise, antipasto, baumkuchen, English muffins, Gruyère cheese, Danish pastry, Canadian bacon, hot tamales, wiener schnitzel, petits fours, spumone, bouillabaisse, maté, scones, Turkish coffee, minestrone, filet mignon."

Immigration plainly was not always a happy experience. It was hard on the newcomers, and hard as well on the communities to which they came. When poor, ill-educated and frightened people disembarked in a strange land, they often fell prey to native racketeers, unscrupulous businessmen and cynical politicians. Boss Tweed said, characteristically, in defense of his own depredations in New York in the 1870's, "This population is too hopelessly split into races and factions to govern it under universal suffrage, except by bribery of patronage, or corruption."

But the very problems of adjustment and assimilation presented a challenge to the American idea—a challenge which subjected that idea to stern testing and eventually brought out the best qualities in American society. Thus the public school became a powerful means of preparing the newcomers for American life. The ideal of the "melting pot" symbolized the process of blending many strains into a single nationality, and we have come to realize in modern times that the "melting pot" need not mean the end of particular ethnic identities or traditions. Only in the case of the Negro has the melting pot failed to bring a minority into the full stream of American life. Today we are belatedly, but resolutely, engaged in ending this condition of national exclusion and shame and abolishing forever the concept of second-class citizenship in the United States.

Sociologists call the process of the melting pot "social mobility." One of America's characteristics has always been the lack of a rigid class structure. It has traditionally been possible for people to move up the social and economic scale. Even if one did not succeed in moving up oneself, there was always the hope that one's children would. Immigration is by definition a gesture of faith in social mobility. It is the expression in action of a positive belief in the possibility of a better life. It has thus contributed greatly to developing the spirit of personal betterment in American society and to strengthening the national confidence in change and the future. Such confidence, when widely shared, sets the national tone. The opportunities that America offered made the dream real, at least for a good many; but the dream itself was in large part the product of millions of plain people beginning a new life in the conviction that life could indeed be better, and each new wave of immigration rekindled the dream.

This is the spirit which so impressed Alexis de Tocqueville, and which he called the spirit of equality. Equality in America has never meant literal equality of condition or capacity; there will always be inequalities in character and ability in any society. Equality has meant rather that, in the words of the Declaration of Independence, "all men are created equal . . . [and] are endowed by their Creator with certain unalienable rights"; it has meant that in a democratic society there should be no inequalities in opportunities or in freedoms. The American philosophy of equality has released the energy of the people, built the economy, subdued the continent, shaped and reshaped the structure of government, and animated the American attitude toward the world outside.

The *continuous* immigration of the nineteenth and early twentieth centuries was thus central to the whole American faith. It gave every old American a standard by which to judge how far he had come and every new American a realization of how far he might go. It reminded every American, old and new, that change is the essence of life, and that American society is a process, not a conclusion. The abundant resources of this land provided the foundation for a great nation. But only people could make the opportunity a reality. Immigration provided the human resources. More than that, it infused the nation with a commitment to far horizons and new frontiers, and thereby kept the pioneer spirit of American life, the spirit of equality and of hope, always alive and strong. "We are the heirs of all time," wrote Herman Melville, "and with all nations we divide our inheritance."

CHAPTER 6

IMMIGRATION POLICY

FROM THE START, IMMIGRATION POLICY HAS BEEN A prominent subject of discussion in America. This is as it must be in a democracy, where every issue should be freely considered and debated.

Immigration, or rather the British policy of clamping down on immigration, was one of the factors behind the colonial desire for independence. Restrictive immigration policies constituted one of the charges against King George III expressed in the Declaration of Independence. And in the Constitutional Convention James Madison noted, "That part of America which has encouraged them [the immigrants] has advanced most rapidly in population, agriculture and the arts." So, too, Washington in his Thanksgiving Day Proclamation of 1795 asked all Americans "humbly and fervently to beseech the kind Author of these blessings . . . to render this country more and more a safe and propitious asylum for the unfortunate of other countries."

Yet there was the basic ambiguity which older Americans

have often shown toward newcomers. In 1797 a member of Congress argued that, while a liberal immigration policy was fine when the country was new and unsettled, now that America had reached its maturity and was fully populated, immigration should stop—an argument which has been repeated at regular intervals throughout American history.

The fear of embroilment in the wars between Britain and France helped the cause of the restrictionists. In 1798 a Federalist Congress passed the Alien Act, authorizing the expulsion of foreigners "dangerous to the peace and safety of the United States" and extending the residence requirement for naturalization from five to fourteen years. But the Alien Act, and its accompanying Sedition Act, went too far. Both acts were allowed to expire in 1801; the naturalization period went back to five years; and President Thomas Jefferson expressed the predominant American sentiment when he asked: "Shall we refuse to the unhappy fugitives from distress that hospitality which the savages of the wilderness extended to our fathers arriving in this land? Shall oppressed humanity find no asylum on this globe?"

But emotions of xenophobia—hatred of foreigners—and of nativism—the policy of keeping America "pure" (that is, of preferring old immigrants to new)—continued to thrive. The increase in the rate of immigration in the 1820's and 1830's set off new waves of hostility, directed especially against the Irish, who, as Catholics, were regarded as members of an alien conspiracy. Even Ralph Waldo Emerson could write to Thomas Carlyle about "the wild Irish element . . . led by Romanish Priests, who sympathize, of course, with despotism." Samuel F. B. Morse, the painter and inventor of the telegraph, wrote an anti-Catholic book entitled *A Foreign Conspiracy Against the Liberties of the United States.* Some alarmed Americans believed that every Catholic was a foreign agent dispatched by the Pope to subvert American society. In 1834 a mob burned down the Ursuline Convent school in Charlestown, Massachusetts. Though the leading citizens of Boston promptly denounced this act, anti-Catholic feeling persisted.

In the 1850's nativism became an open political movement. A secret patriotic society, the Order of the Star-Spangled Banner, founded about 1850, grew into the American party, whose members were pledged to vote only for native Americans, to demand a twenty-one-year naturalization period and to fight Roman Catholicism. When asked about their program, they were instructed to answer, "I know nothing about it," so people called them the Know-Nothings. Coming into existence at a time when the slavery issue was dissolving the older party allegiances, the Know-Nothings for a moment attracted considerable support. They elected six state governors and seventy-five Congressmen in 1854 and got almost 25 percent of the vote for their candidate, former President Millard Fillmore, in 1856. But soon they, too, were split by the slavery issue, and the party vanished as quickly as it had appeared.

The legacy of the Know-Nothings lived beyond its life as an organization. The seeds of bigotry, fear and hatred bore fruit again in the years after the Civil War. The Ku Klux Klan launched a campaign of terrorism against the Negroes, and in the 1890's the American Protective Association tried to revive popular feeling against Catholics. Other nativists began to turn their attention to the Jews. In the meantime, agitators on the West Coast denounced the "yellow peril," and Congress in 1882 passed the first of a number of laws banning Oriental immigration. Yet, except for Oriental exclusion, Congress ignored the nativist clamor, and most Americans regarded nativism with abhorrence. When a Protestant clergyman supporting James G. Blaine in 1884 denounced the Democrats as the party of "rum, Romanism and rebellion," he provoked a reaction which may well have lost the election for Blaine, who himself had a mother of Irish Catholic descent.

The First World War led to another outbreak of nativism. A new group, adopting the program of the Know-Nothings and the name of the Ku Klux Klan, came into being, denouncing everything its members disliked—Negroes, Catholics, Jews, evolutionists, religious liberals, internationalists, pacifists—in the name of true Americanism and of "Nordic superiority." For a season, the new KKK prospered, claiming five million members, mostly in the South but also in Indiana, Ohio, Kansas and Maine. But, like the other nativist movements, the fall of the Klan was as dramatic as its rise. It died when a genuine crisis, the depression, turned people's attention away from the phony issue of racism to the real problems facing the nation. In later years, the Jew succeeded the Catholic as the chief target of nativist hysteria, and some Catholics, themselves so recently persecuted, now regrettably joined in the attack on the newer minorities.

America had no cause to be smug about the failure of these movements to take deep root. Nativism failed, not because the seeds were not there to be cultivated, but because American society is too complex for an agitation so narrowly and viciously conceived to be politically successful. That the nativist movements found any response at all must cause us to look searchingly at ourselves. That the response was at times so great offers cause for alarm.

Still it remains a remarkable fact that, except for the Oriental Exclusion Act, there was no governmental response till after the First World War.

Not only were newcomers allowed to enter freely, but in some periods they were actively sought after.

Inevitably, though, this mass influx of people presented problems which the federal government was forced to recognize. In 1882, recognizing the need for a national immigration policy, Congress enacted the first general legislation on the subject. The most important aspect of this law was that, for the first time, the government undertook to exclude certain classes of undesirables, such as lunatics, convicts, idiots and persons likely to become public charges. In 1891 certain health standards were added as well as a provision excluding polygamists.

From time to time additional laws were added. The only deviation from the basic policy of free, nondiscriminatory immigration was the Oriental Exclusion Act.

Under a special treaty arrangement with China, nationals of that country had been guaranteed free and unrestricted immigration to the United States. At the peak of that immigration, in 1882, there were only forty thousand arrivals; even in 1890 there were but 107,000 Chinese in America. Most of them lived in California and had proved good and useful workers and citizens. Although they had originally been welcomed to America for their services in building railroads and reclaiming the land, the conviction began to grow that Chinese labor was undermining the standards of "American" labor. This became virtually an obsession with many people. In the early 1870's anti-Chinese agitation in California became organized and focused under the leadership of Denis Kearney, who was, ironically, an immigrant from Ireland. A campaign of organized violence against Chinese communities took form, and the hysteria led to political pressure too violent to be resisted. President Hayes vetoed an act of Congress restricting Chinese immigration, but he did force renegotiation of the Burlingame Treaty under which the government of China agreed to restrict emigration voluntarily. Not satisfied with this remedy, Congress then enacted and the President signed into law a series of measures shutting off almost completely immigration from China.

Shameful as these episodes were, they were, however, only an exception to the prevailing policy. A more serious warning of things to come was sounded in 1897 when Congress, for the first time, provided a literacy test for adult immigrants. President Cleveland vetoed the measure. Presidents Taft and Wilson vetoed similar bills on the ground that literacy was a test only of educational opportunity and not of a person's ability or his potential worth as a citizen. In 1917, with tension high because of the war, Congress overrode President Wilson's veto and the literacy test became law.

The twenty-year fight over the literacy test can now be seen as a significant turning point in immigration policy. Indeed, many saw it as such at that time. Finley Peter Dunne, creator of the immortal Mr. Dooley, devoted one of Mr. Dooley's dissertations in 1902 to the subject of the test and immigration. With magnificent irony the Irish bartender says, "As a pilgrim father that missed the first boat, I must raise me claryon voice again' the invasion iv this fair land be th' paupers an' arnychists in Europe. Ye bet I must—because I'm here first. . . . In thim days America was th' refuge iv th' oppressed in all th' wurruld. . . . But as I tell ye, 'tis diff'rent now. 'Tis time we put our back again' th' open dure an' keep out th' savage horde."

But there is no denying the fact that by the turn of the century the opinion was becoming widespread that the numbers of new immigrants should be limited. Those who were opposed to all immigration and all "foreigners" were now joined by those who believed sincerely, and with some basis in fact, that America's capacity to absorb immigration was limited. This movement toward restricting immigration represented a social and economic reaction, not only to the tremendous increase in immigration after 1880, but also to the shift in its main sources, to Southern, Eastern and Southeastern Europe.

Anti-immigration sentiment was heightened by World War I, and the disillusionment and strong wave of isolationism that marked its aftermath. It was in this climate, in 1921, that Congress passed and the President signed the first major law in our country's history severely limiting new immigration by establishing an emergency quota system. An era in American history had ended; we were committed to a radically new policy toward the peopling of the nation.

The Act of 1921 was an early version of the so-called "national origins" system. Its provisions limited immigration of numbers of each nationality to a certain percentage of the number of foreign-born individuals of that nationality resident in the United States according to the 1910 census.

Nationality meant country of birth. The total number of immigrants permitted to enter under this system each year was 357,000.

In 1924 the Act was revised, creating a temporary arrangement for the years 1924 to 1929, under which the national quotas for 1924 were equal to 2 percent of the number of foreign-born persons of a given nationality living in the United States in 1890, or about 164,000 people. The permanent system, which went into force in 1929, includes essentially all the elements of immigration policy that are in our law today. The immigration statutes now establish a system of annual quotas to govern immigration from each country. Under this system 156,987 quota immigrants are permitted to enter the United States each year. The quotas from each country are based upon the national origins of the population of the United States in 1920.

The use of the year 1920 is arbitrary. It rests upon the fact that this system was introduced in 1924 and the last prior census was in 1920. The use of a national origins system is without basis in either logic or reason. It neither satisfies a national need nor accomplishes an international purpose. In an age of interdependence among nations such a system is an anachronism, for it discriminates among applicants for admission into the United States on the basis of accident of birth.

Because of the composition of our population in 1920, the system is heavily weighted in favor of immigration from Northern Europe and severely limits immigration from Southern and Eastern Europe and from other parts of the world.

To cite some recent examples: Great Britain has an annual quota of 65,361 immigration visas and used 28,291 of them. Germany has a quota of 25,814 and used 26,533 (of this number, about one-third are wives of servicemen who could enter on a nonquota basis). Ireland's quota is 17,756 and only 6,054 Irish availed themselves of it. On the other hand, Poland is permitted 6,488, and there is a backlog of 61,293 Poles wishing to enter the United States. Italy is permitted 5,666 and has a backlog of 132,435. Greece's quota is 308; her backlog is 96,538. Thus a Greek citizen desiring to emigrate to this country has little chance of coming here. And an American citizen with a Greek father or mother must wait at least eighteen months to bring his parents here to join him. A citizen whose married son or daughter, or brother or sister, is Italian cannot obtain a quota number for them for two years or more. Meanwhile, many thousands of quota numbers are wasted because they are not wanted or needed by nationals of the countries to which they are assigned.

In short, a qualified person born in England or Ireland who wants to emigrate to the United States can do so at any time. A person born in Italy, Hungary, Poland or the Baltic States may have to wait many years before his turn is reached. This system is based upon the assumption that there is some reason for keeping the origins of our population in exactly the same proportions as they existed in 1920. Such an idea is at complete variance with the American traditions and principles that the qualifications of an immigrant do not depend upon his country of birth, and violates the spirit expressed in the Declaration of Independence that "all men are created equal."

One writer has listed six motives behind the Act of 1924. They were: (1) postwar isolationism; (2) the doctrine of the alleged superiority of Anglo-Saxon and Teutonic "races"; (3) the fear that "pauper labor" would lower wage levels; (4) the belief that people of certain nations were less law-abiding than others; (5) the fear of foreign ideologies and subversion; (6) the fear that entrance of too many people with different customs and habits would undermine our national and social unity and order. All of these arguments can be found in Congressional debates on the subject and may be heard today in discussions over a new national policy toward immigration. Thus far, they have prevailed. The policy of 1924 was continued in all its essentials by the Immigration and Nationality Act of 1952.

There have been some minor amendments to that Act. In 1957 legislation was passed to reunite families being separated by restrictive provisions of the immigration legislation. Under it approximately eighty thousand persons have been admitted. Among them are the wives, husbands, parents or children of American citizens, or escapees and refugees from Communist persecution. In 1958 the immigration laws were amended to give the Attorney General added discretionary powers to adjust the status of people admitted as aliens. A 1959 amendment further facilitated the reunion of families, and a 1960 amendment provided for United States participation in the resettlement of certain refugee-escapees. In 1961 a special status was granted orphans coming to this country for adoption by American parents.

CHAPTER 7

WHERE WE STAND

THE IMMIGRATION AND NATIONALITY ACT OF 1952 undertook to codify all our national laws on immigration. This was a proper and long overdue task. But it was not just a housekeeping chore. In the course of the deliberation over the Act, many basic decisions about our immigration policy were made. The total racial bar against the naturalization of Japanese, Koreans and other East Asians was removed, and a minimum annual quota of one hundred was provided for each of these countries. Provision was also made to make it easier to reunite husbands and wives. Most important of all was the decision to do nothing about the national origins system.

The famous words of Emma Lazarus on the pedestal of the Statue of Liberty read: "Give me your tired, your poor, your huddled masses yearning to breathe free." Until 1921 this was an accurate picture of our society. Under present law it would be appropriate to add: "as long as they come from Northern Europe, are not too tired or too poor or slightly ill, never stole a loaf of bread, never joined any questionable organization, and can document their activities for the past two years."

Furthermore, the national origins quota system has strong overtones of an indefensible racial preference. It is strongly weighted toward so-called Anglo-Saxons, a phrase which one writer calls "a term of art" encompassing almost anyone from Northern and Western Europe. Sinclair Lewis described his hero, Martin Arrowsmith, this way: "a typical pure-bred-Anglo-Saxon American—which means that he was a union of German, French, Scotch-Irish, perhaps a little Spanish, conceivably of the strains lumped together as 'Jewish,' and a great deal of English, which is itself a combination of primitive Britain, Celt, Phoenician, Roman, German, Dane and Swede."

Yet, however much our present policy may be deplored, it still remains our national policy. As President Truman said when he vetoed the Immigration and Nationality Act (only to have that veto overridden): "The idea behind this discriminatory policy was, to put it baldly, that Americans with English or Irish names were better people and better citizens than Americans with Italian or Greek or Polish names. . . . Such a concept is utterly unworthy of our traditions and our ideals."

Partly as a result of the inflexibility of the national origins quota system, the government has had to resort to temporary expedients to meet emergency situations. The 1957 Kennedy amendment, which permitted alien spouses, parents and children with inconsequential disqualifications to enter the United States, was responsive to this need. In 1948 Congress passed the Displaced Persons Act allowing more than 400,000 people made homeless by the war to come to this country. In 1953 Congress passed the Refugee Relief Act to admit about

200,000 people, most of whom had fled from behind the Iron Curtain. Under this Act and under a clause of the Immigration and Nationality Act of 1952, not originally intended for use in such situations, some thirty thousand Freedom Fighters from Hungary were admitted in 1957. As a result it became necessary to pass a special law in 1958 to regularize the status of many of these immigrants.

Following the 1958 earthquakes in the Azores which left so many Portuguese homeless, none of these people could enter the United States as quota immigrants. Persons of Dutch origin in the Netherlands who were displaced from Indonesia were also ineligible to enter the United States as quota immigrants. Both needs were met by the Pastore-Kennedy-Walter Act of 1958 admitting a number of them on a nonquota basis into the United States. In 1962 a special law had to be passed to permit the immigration of several thousand Chinese refugees who had escaped from Communist China to Hong Kong. The same legislative procedure was used as in the 1957 Hungarian program. Each world crisis is met by a new exception to the Immigration and Nationality Act of 1952. Each exception reflects the natural humanitarian impulses of the American people, which is in keeping with our traditions of shelter to the homeless and refuge for the oppressed.

While none of these measures are, of themselves, especially generous responses to the tremendous problems to which they are addressed, they all have a great impact on our foreign policy. They demonstrate that there is still a place in America for people fleeing from tyranny or natural calamity. Nevertheless, the effect of these actions is diluted by the very fact that they are viewed as exceptions to our national policy rather than as a part of that policy.

Another measure of the inadequacy of the Immigration and Nationality Act has been the huge volume of private immigration bills introduced in Congress. These are bills to deal with individual hardship cases for which the general law fails to provide. In the Eighty-seventh Congress over 3,500 such bills were introduced. Private immigration bills make up about half of our legislation today.

It is not hard to see why. A poor European college girl was convicted three times for putting slugs in a pay telephone, and fifteen years later, married to an American teacher abroad, she was denied entrance to our country because of three separate convictions for a crime involving moral turpitude. Or another case: An Italian immigrant living in Massachusetts with his small children could not bring his wife to the United States because she had been convicted on two counts involving moral turpitude. Her crimes? In 1913 and 1939 she had stolen bundles of sticks to build a fire. It took acts of Congress to reunite both these families.

These are examples of the inadequacies of the present law. They are important of themselves because people's lives are affected by them. But they are more important for what they represent of the way America looks at the world and the way America looks at itself.

There is, of course, a legitimate argument for some limitation upon immigration. We no longer need settlers for virgin lands, and our economy is expanding more slowly than in the nineteenth and early twentieth centuries. A superficial analysis of the heated arguments over immigration policy which have taken place since 1952 might give the impression that there was an irreconcilable conflict, as if one side wanted to go back to the policy of our founding fathers, of unrestricted immigration, and the other side wanted to stop all further immigration. In fact, there are only a few basic differences between the most liberal bill offered in recent years, sponsored by former Senator Herbert H. Lehman, and the supporters of the status quo. The present law admits 156,700 quota immigrants annually. The Lehman bill (like a bill introduced by Senator Philip A. Hart and cosponsored by over one-third of the members of the Senate) would admit 250,000.

The clash of opinion arises not over the number of immigrants to be admitted, but over the test for admission—the national origins quota system. Instead of using the discriminatory test of where the immigrant was born, the reform proposals would base admission on the immigrant's possession of skills our country needs and on the humanitarian ground of reuniting families. Such legislation does not seek to make over the face of America. Immigrants would still be given tests for health, intelligence, morality and security.

The force of this argument is recognized by the special measures enacted since 1952 which have ignored the established pattern of favoring Northern and Western Europe immigration over Southern and Eastern European countries. These statutes have resulted in the admission of a great many more persons from Southern European countries than would have been possible under the McCarran-Walter Act.

But more than a decade has elapsed since the last substantial amendment to these laws. There is a compelling need for Congress to re-examine and make changes in them.

Religious and civic organizations, ethnic associations and newspaper editorials, citizens from every walk of life and groups of every description have expressed their support for a more rational and less prejudiced immigration law. Congressional leaders of both parties have urged the adoption of new legislation that would eliminate the most objectionable features of the McCarran-Walter Act and the nationalities quota system.

It is not only the initial assignment of quota numbers which is arbitrary and unjust; additional inequity results from the failure of the law to permit full utilization of the authorized quota numbers. The tiny principality of Andorra in the Pyrenees Mountains, with 6,500 Spanish-speaking inhabitants, has an American immigration quota of 100, while Spain, with 28 million people, has a quota of only 250. While American citizens wait for years for their relatives to receive a quota, approximately sixty thousand numbers are wasted each year because the countries to which they are assigned have far more numbers allocated to them than they have emigrants seeking to move to the United States. There is no way at present in which these numbers can be reassigned to nations where immense backlogs of applicants for admission to the United States have accumulated. This deficiency in the law should be corrected.

A special discriminatory formula is now applied to the immigration of persons who are attributable by their ancestry to an area called the Asia-Pacific triangle. This area embraces all countries from Pakistan to Japan and the Pacific islands north of Australia and New Zealand. Usually, the quota under which a prospective immigrant must enter is determined by his place of birth. However, if as much as one-half of an immigrant's ancestors came from nations in the Asia-Pacific triangle, he must rely upon the small quota assigned to the country of his ancestry, regardless of where he was born. This provision of the law should be repealed.

The Presidential message to Congress of July 23, 1963, recommended that the national origins system be replaced by a formula governing immigration to the United States which takes into account: (1) the skills of the immigrant and their relationship to our needs; (2) the family relationship between immigrants and persons already here, so that the reuniting of families is encouraged; and (3) the priority of registration. Present law grants a preference to immigrants with special skills, education or training. It also grants a preference to various relatives of the United States citizens and lawfully resident aliens. But it does so only within a national origins quota. It should be modified so that those with the greatest ability to add to the national welfare, no matter where they are born, are granted the highest priority. The next priority should go to those who seek to be reunited with their relatives. For applicants with equal claims, the earliest registrant should be the first admitted.

In order to remove other existing barriers to the reuniting of families, two additional improvements in the law are needed.

First, parents of American citizens, who now have a preferred quota status, should be accorded nonquota status.

Second, parents of aliens resident in the United States, who now have no preference, should be accorded a preference, after skilled specialists and other relatives of citizens and alien residents.

These changes will have little effect on the number of immigrants admitted. They will have a major effect insofar as they relieve the hardship many of our citizens and residents now face in being separated from their parents.

These changes will not solve all the problems of immigration. But they will insure that progress will continue to be made toward our ideals and toward the realization of humanitarian objectives.

We must avoid what the Irish poet John Boyle O'Reilly once called

Organized charity, scrimped and iced,
In the name of a cautious, statistical Christ.

Immigration policy should be generous; it should be fair; it should be flexible. With such a policy we can turn to the world, and to our own past, with clean hands and a clear conscience. Such a policy would be but a reaffirmation of old principles. It would be an expression of our agreement with George Washington that "The bosom of America is open to receive not only the opulent and respectable stranger, but the oppressed and persecuted of all nations and religions; whom we shall welcome to a participation of all our rights and privileges, if by decency and propriety of conduct they appear to merit the enjoyment."

APPENDIX A

THE UNITED STATES OF AMERICA— A NATION OF IMMIGRANTS

THE MAP ON THE FOLLOWING PAGES INDICATES THE general distribution of immigrant groups in the United States. All told, more than 42 million immigrants have come to our shores since the beginning of our history as a nation. Why they came here and what they did after they arrived make up the story of America. They came for a variety of reasons from every quarter of the world, representing almost every race, almost every religion, and almost every creed. Through their ingenuity, their industry and their imagination, they were able to create out of a wilderness a thriving and prosperous nation—and, through their dedication to liberty and freedom, they helped to build a government reflecting man's most cherished ideals.

- From Great Britain came Pilgrims, who sought freedom; Quakers, who loved their brothers but who were not allowed to love them in peace; sturdy Scots and

Welsh. To date, estimated immigration from Great Britain: 4,642,096. Peak year: 1888.

- The bold, imaginative Irish left their land during the years of famine for the land of opportunity. Estimated immigration from Ireland to date: 4,693,009. Peak decade: 1851–60.

- From Germany came the liberals and those who fled persecution. Estimated immigration from Germany to date: 6,798,313. Peak decade: 1881–90.

- Fleeing Czarist and Communist suppression, came an estimated 3,344,998 Russians, some 40 percent of them Jews fleeing persecution. Peak decade: 1901–10.

- Frenchmen cried, "Let us rule ourselves; our kings are not divine!" To date, estimated immigration from France: 698,188. Peak year: 1851.

- The Japanese and Chinese brought their gentle dreams to the West Coast. To date, estimated immigration from Japan: 338,087. Peak year: 1907. Estimated immigration from China: 411,585. Peak year: 1882.

- The Greeks found soil where vineyards might flourish. To date, estimated immigration from Greece: 499,465. Peak year: 1907.

- In Poland they heard of the land where freedom is. To date, estimated immigration from Poland: 451,010. Peak year: 1921.

- From Austria-Hungary and Rumania whole villages banded together to find a new life. To date, estimated immigration from Austria and Hungary: 4,280,863. Peak year: 1907. To date, estimated immigration from Rumania: 159,497. Peak year: 1921.

- Italians settled in the cities of the East and the valleys of the West. To date, estimated immigration from Italy: 5,017,625. Peak year: 1907.
- To the Midwest the Scandinavians brought their knowledge of agriculture. To date, estimated immigration from Denmark: 354,331. Peak year: 1882. From Finland: 28,358. Peak year: 1902. From Norway: 843,867. Peak year: 1882. From Sweden: 1,255,296. Peak year: 1882.

These are some of yesterday's immigrants who have supplied a continuous flow of creative abilities and ideas that have enriched our nation.

The immigrants we welcome today and tomorrow will carry on this tradition and help us to retain, reinvigorate and strengthen the American spirit.

A NATION

ALASKA

Pacific Ocean

JAPANESE NORWEGIANS SWEDISH FINNISH
WASHINGTON

JAPANESE NORWEGIANS SWEDISH FINNISH
OREGON
SPANISH

IDAHO
ENGLISH SWISS

MONTANA
YUGOSLAVS

NORTH DAKOTA
RUSSIANS NORWEGIANS GERMANS SWEDISH

SOUTH DAKOTA
DANISH DUTCH GERMAN

WYOMING
SCOTS ENGLISH

NEBRASKA
CZECHOSLOVAKS GERMANS

RUSSIANS SWISS ITALIANS FRENCH JAPANESE
CALI~ FORNIA
ARMENIANS CHINESE MEXICANS SPANISH

NEVADA
IRISH FRENCH SWISS

SWISS ENGLISH DANISH SCOTS SWEDISH DUTCH
UTAH
SALT

COLORADO
GERMANS SPANISH

KANSAS
GERMANS

MEXICANS SPANISH
ARIZONA

NEW MEXICO
SPANISH MEXICANS

OKLAHOMA
ENGLISH GERMANS

HAWAII
CHINESE JAPANESE

TEX
SPANIS FRENC MEXICA

Appendix B

CHRONOLOGY OF IMMIGRATION

1607	Founding of Virginia by English colonists, to "fetch treasure" and enjoy "religious and happy government."
1619	First shipload of twenty Negro slaves arrives at Jamestown.
1620	Voyage of the *Mayflower,* carrying Pilgrims who welcome opportunity of "advancing the gospel of . . . Christ in those remote parts of the world."
1623	Settlement of New Netherland as a trading post by Dutch West India Company.
1630–40	Puritans migrate to New England to establish a form of government that will allow them to worship as they desire.
1634	Lord Baltimore founds Maryland as a refuge for English Catholics.
1642	Outbreak of English Civil War and decrease in Puritan migration.

1649   Passage of Maryland Toleration Act, extending toleration to all bodies professing trinitarian Christianity.

1654   First Jewish immigrants to reach North America arrive at New Amsterdam fleeing Portuguese persecution in Brazil.

1660   Emigration from England officially discouraged by government of Charles II, acting on mercantilist doctrine that the wealth of a country depends on number of its inhabitants.

1670   Settlement of the Carolinas by a group of English courtiers, anxious to promote national self-sufficiency—and their own fortunes.

1681   Founding of Pennsylvania by the Quakers, as William Penn's "holy experiment" in universal philanthropy and brotherhood.

1683   First German settlers, Mennonites, to reach New World arrive in Pennsylvania, in a desire to withdraw from the world and live peaceably according to the tenets of their faith.

1685   Revocation of Edict of Nantes by Louis XIV, culmination of growth of religious intolerance in France, leads to arrival of small but important group of Huguenots. Most settle in South Carolina.

1697   Royal African Company's monopoly of slave trade ends and the business of slavery expands rapidly. New Englanders find it extremely profitable.

1707   Act of Union between England and Scotland begins a new era of Scottish migration. Scots settle as merchants and factors in colonial seaports; lowland artisans and laborers leave Glasgow to become indentured servants in tobacco colonies and New York.

1709   Exodus from German Palatinate in wake of devastation wreaked by wars of Louis XIV. Palatines settle in Hudson Valley and Pennsylvania.

1717   Act of English Parliament legalizes transportation to American colonies as punishment; contractors begin regular shipments from jails, most (of some 30,000) to Virginia and Maryland.

1718   Large-scale Scotch-Irish immigration begins, sparked by discontent with Old Country land system: absentee landlords, high rents, short leases. Most settle first in New England, then in Maryland and Pennsylvania.

1730   Colonization of Virginia valley and Carolina back country by Germans (Pietist and pacifist sectarians) and Scotch-Irish from Pennsylvania.

1732   Georgia founded by James Oglethorpe, as a buffer against Spanish and French attack, as a producer of raw silk and as a haven for imprisoned debtors. (Silk scheme fails; only a handful of debtors come.)

1740   Parliament enacts Naturalization Act conferring British citizenship on alien immigrants to colonies in hope of encouraging Jewish immigration. Jews enjoy a greater degree of political and religious freedom in the American colonies than anywhere in the world.

1745   Jacobite rebellion in Scotland to put Stuarts
            back on throne fails. Some rebels transported
            to American colonies as punishment.

1755   Expulsion of French Acadians from Nova Sco-
            tia on suspicion of disloyalty. Survivors settle in
            Louisiana.

1771–73   Depression in Ulster linen trade and acute
            agrarian crisis bring new influx of Scotch-Irish,
            around 10,000 annually.

1775   British Government suspends emigration on
            outbreak of hostilities in the American colonies.

1783   Treaty of Paris ends Revolutionary War. Re-
            vival of immigration; most numerous group:
            Scotch-Irish.

1789   Outbreak of French Revolution. Emigration
            to the United States of aristocrats and royalist
            sympathizers.

1791   Negro revolt in Santo Domingo; 10,000–
            20,000 French exiles take refuge in the United
            States, principally in towns on the Atlantic sea-
            board.

1793   Wars of the French Revolution send Girondists
            and Jacobins threatened by guillotine to the
            United States.

1798   Unsuccessful Irish rebellion; rebels emigrate
            to U.S., as do distressed artisans and yeoman
            farmers and agricultural laborers depressed by
            bad harvests and low prices.

            Alien and Sedition Acts give President ar-
            bitrary powers to seize and expel resident aliens

suspected of engaging in subversive activities. Though never invoked, Acts induce several ship-loads of Frenchmen to return to France and Santo Domingo.

1803   Resumption of war between England and France. Disruption of transatlantic trade; emigration from continental Europe practically impossible.

British Passenger Act limits numbers to be carried by emigrant ships, effectively checks Irish emigration.

1807   Congress prohibits importing of Negro slaves into the U.S. (prohibited by Delaware in 1776; Virginia, 1778; Maryland, 1783; South Carolina, 1787; North Carolina, 1794; Georgia, 1798; reopened by South Carolina in 1803).

1812   War of 1812 brings immigration to a complete halt.

1814   Treaty of Ghent ends War of 1812. Beginning of first great wave of immigration: 5,000,000 immigrants between 1815 and 1860.

1818   Black Ball Line of sailing packets begins regular Liverpool–New York service; Liverpool becomes main port of departure for Irish and British, as well as considerable numbers of Germans and Norwegians.

1825   Great Britain repeals laws prohibiting emigration as ineffective; official endorsement of view that England is overpopulated.

Arrival in U.S. of first group of Norwegian immigrants in sloop *Restaurationen,* consisting of freeholders leaving an overpopulated country and shrunken farms. They are followed by cotters, laborers and servants.

1830   Polish revolution. Thirty-six sections of public land in Illinois allotted by Congress to Polish revolutionary refugees.

1837   Financial panic. Nativists complain that immigration lowers wage levels, contributes to the decline of the apprenticeship system and generally depresses the condition of labor.

1840   Cunard Line founded. Beginning of era of steamship lines especially designed for passenger transportation between Europe and the United States.

1845   Native American party founded, with minimal support in fourteen states; precursor of nativist, anti-immigrant Know-Nothing party which reached its peak in 1855, when it elected six governors, dominated several state legislatures and sent a sizable delegation to Congress.

1846   Crop failures in Germany and Holland. Mortgage foreclosures and forced sales send tens of thousands of dispossessed to U.S.

1846–47   Irish Potato Famine. Large-scale emigration to the United States of all classes of Irish population, not only laborers and cotters, but even substantial farmers.

1848   Revolution in Germany. Failure of revolution results in emigration of political refugees to America.

1855	Opening of Castle Garden immigrant depot in New York City to process mass immigration.
1856	Collapse of Know-Nothing movement in Presidential election; candidate Millard Fillmore carries only one state.
	Irish Catholic Colonization Convention at Buffalo, New York, to promote Irish rural colonization in the U.S. Strongly opposed by Eastern bishops, movement proves unsuccessful.
1861–65	Large numbers of immigrants serve on both sides during American Civil War.
1882	First federal immigration law bars lunatics, idiots, convicts and those likely to become public charges.
	Chinese Exclusion Act denies entry to Chinese laborers for a period of ten years (renewed in 1892; Chinese immigration suspended indefinitely in 1902; many return home).
	Outbreak of anti-Semitism in Russia; sharp rise in Jewish migration to U.S.
1885	Foran Act prohibits importing of contract labor, but not of skilled labor for new industries, artists, actors, lecturers, domestic servants; individuals in U.S. not to be prevented from assisting immigration of relatives and personal friends.
1886	Statue of Liberty dedicated, just when the resistance to unrestricted immigration begins to mount.
1890	Superintendent of the Census announces disappearance of the frontier.

1891   Congress adds health qualifications to immi-
            gration restrictions.

            Pogroms in Russia. Large Jewish immigra-
            tion to U.S.

1892   Ellis Island replaces Castle Garden as a recep-
            tion center for immigrants.

1893   Economic depression brings a vast accession of
            strength to anti-Catholic American Protective
            Association.

1894   Immigration Restriction League organized, to
            be the spearhead of restrictionist movement for
            next twenty-five years. Emphasizes distinction
            between "old" (Northern and Western Euro-
            pean) and "new" (Southern and Eastern Euro-
            pean) immigrants.

1894–96   Massacres of Armenian Christians by Moslems
            set emigration to U.S. in motion.

1897   Literacy test for immigrants vetoed by Presi-
            dent Cleveland.

1903   Immigration law denies entry, *inter alia,* to an-
            archists or persons believing in the overthrow
            by force or violence of the government of the
            U.S., or any government, or in the assassina-
            tion of public officials (as a result of President
            McKinley's assassination by the American-
            born anarchist Leon Czolgosz).

1905   Japanese and Korean Exclusion League, re-
            named the Asiatic Exclusion League in 1907,
            formed by organized labor in protest against
            the influx of immigrant laborers from Asia and

Southeast Asia and in fear of threat to the living standards of American workers.

1907–08   Gentleman's agreement, whereby Japanese Government undertakes to deny passports to laborers going directly from Japan to U.S., fails to satisfy West Coast exclusionists.

1913   California legislature passes Alien Land Law, effectively barring Japanese, as "aliens ineligible for citizenship," from owning agricultural land in the state.

1914–18   World War I. End of period of mass migration to the U.S.

1916   Madison Grant's *The Passing of the Great Race* calls for exclusion, on racist grounds, of "inferior" Alpine, Mediterranean and Jewish "breeds."

1917   Literacy test for immigrants finally adopted after being defeated in Congress in 1896, 1898, 1902, 1906, vetoed in 1897 by President Cleveland, in 1913 by President Taft, and in 1915 and 1917 by President Wilson. It was passed by overriding the second veto by President Wilson.

1919   Big Red Scare: anti-foreign fears and hatreds transferred from German Americans to alien revolutionaries and radicals. Thousands of alien radicals seized in Palmer Raids, hundreds deported.

1921   Emergency immigration restriction law introduces quota system, heavily weighted in favor of natives of Northern and Western Europe, all but

	slamming the door on Southern and Eastern Europeans. Immediate slump in immigration.
1923	Ku Klux Klan, at heart a virulently anti-immigrant movement, reaches its peak strength.
1924	National Origins Act adopted, settling ceiling on number of immigrants, and establishing discriminatory national-racial quotas.
1929	National Origins Act becomes operative. Stock market crash. Demands that immigration be further reduced during economic crisis lead Hoover administration to order rigorous enforcement of prohibition against admission of persons liable to be public charges.
1933	Hitler becomes German chancellor; anti-Semitic campaign begins. Jewish refugees from Nazi Germany come to U.S., though barriers imposed by the quota system are not lifted.
1934	Philippine Independence Act restricts Filipino immigration to an annual quota of fifty.
1939	World War II begins.
1941	U.S. enters war. All immigrant groups support united war effort.
1942	Evacuation of Japanese-Americans from Pacific Coast to detention camps, victims of deep-seated suspicion and animosity, and unjustified fear of espionage and sabotage.
1945	Large-scale Puerto Rican migration to escape poverty on island. Many settle in New York.
1946	War Brides Act provides for admission of foreign-born wives of American servicemen.

1948	Displaced Persons Act (amended in 1950) provides for admission of 400,000 refugees during a four-year period; three-quarters regular displaced persons from countries with low quotas, one-quarter *Volksdeutsche* (ethnic Germans), special groups of Greek, Polish and Italian refugees, orphans and European refugees stranded in the Far East.
1952	Immigration and Naturalization Act, codifying existing legislation, makes the quota system even more rigid and repressive, except for a token quota granted those in the Asia-Pacific triangle.
1953–56	Refugee Relief Act grants visas to some 5,000 Hungarians after 1956 revolution; President Eisenhower invites 30,000 more to come in on parole.
1954	Ellis Island closed. Symbol of ending of mass migration.
1957	Special legislation to admit Hungarian refugees.
1959	Castro revolution successful in Cuba.
1960	Cuban refugees paroled into U.S.
1962	Special permission for admission of refugees from Hong Kong.
1963	Congress urged by President Kennedy to pass new legislation eliminating national origins quota system.

MAJOR IMMIGRATION POLICY DEVELOPMENTS AFTER 1963

PRESIDENT JOHN F. KENNEDY REVISED AND EXPANDED *A Nation of Immigrants* shortly before his assassination on November 22, 1963, in Dallas, Texas.

1965	President Johnson signed into law an immigration bill that abolished the restrictive national origins quota system that discriminated against Southern Europeans and Asians. The quota system apportioned the number of people allowed to immigrate to the United States each year to countries according to its natives or descendants in the country as represented in the census of 1920. The quota system was phased out over the succeeding three years.
1966	The Cuban Adjustment Act provided permanent residence to Cubans admitted into the United States after January 1, 1959.

1969   President Nixon signed into law a bill amending the Immigration and Nationality Act by removing its prohibition against acquiring citizenship within 60 days prior to a general election.

1971   The U.S. Supreme Court ruled that states could not deny welfare benefits to needy immigrants.

1972   The U.S. State Department issued a set of guidelines for dealing with requests for asylum to bring to every echelon of government "a sense of the depth and urgency of our commitment."

The Commission on Population Growth and the American Future, established by Congress in 1970, urged a crackdown on "illegal immigration" and recommended that legal immigration not exceed the current levels.

1973   The U.S. Supreme Court invalidated a New York civil service law barring permanent employment to non-citizens.

1974   The U.S. Supreme Court upheld Immigration and Naturalization Service rules permitting Canadians and Mexicans to commute freely into the United States to perform daily or seasonal jobs.

1975   The Ford administration's budget to Congress called for an increase in projected spending to curb "illegal immigration."

The U.S. Supreme Court ruled that the Border Patrol could not stop a car and question its occupants about their immigration status solely because they were of Mexican ancestry.

1976 President Ford signed into law a bill revising procedures governing immigration from Western Hemisphere countries, eliminating preferential treatment and bringing such immigration into line with procedures for Eastern Hemisphere immigration.

1977 The Justice Department approved entry to the United States of five thousand Soviet Jewish immigrants eligible to enter the country but not admitted because of limits set by immigration laws.

1978 Hundreds of Haitian refugees entered the United States after the government of the Bahamas ordered them to leave or face deportation.

 The caps limiting the number of immigrants from the respective Eastern and Western hemispheres were abolished in favor of a worldwide ceiling.

1979 The Justice Department told the Immigration and Naturalization Service to enforce a statutory ban on admission into the United States based on an immigrant's sexual orientation.

1980 The Refugee Act of 1980 systematizes the refugee process and codifies asylum status. Ten million permanent immigrants are admitted legally to the United States. The act was enacted in response to the Vietnamese and Cuban refugee crisis.

1984   The U.S. Supreme Court narrowed a residency deportation provision of the Immigration and Nationality Act by holding seven years of continuous physical presence in the United States to be a precondition for suspension of deportation procedures.

1986   President Reagan signed into law a major revision of U.S. immigration laws which he hailed as "the most comprehensive reform of our immigration laws since 1952." The law, five years in the making, offered amnesty and legal residency to millions of undocumented immigrants living in the United States and sought to curtail "illegal immigration."

1988   The U.S.'s amnesty program for illegal immigrants expired as applicants jammed legalization centers. More than 1.4 million undocumented immigrants sought amnesty by claiming residence in the United States since at least 1982.

1990   President George H. W. Bush signed into law the Immigration Act of 1990 which he called the "most comprehensive reform of our immigration laws in sixty-six years." The act increased legal immigration ceilings and employment-based immigration, emphasizing skills. The 1924 law established country-by-country quotas, which were eliminated in 1965 when the system was oriented toward admission on the basis of skills and family reunification.

A change to the 1952 Immigration and

Nationality Act barred the State Department from excluding any person from the United States for beliefs, statements, or political associations for which American citizens would be protected under the Constitution.

1993   A *New York Times/CBS News* poll found that 61 percent of Americans surveyed favored a decrease in immigration, which reflected a continuing trend of opinion less favorable to immigration.

1994   The Immigration and Naturalization Service instituted a fast-track handling of asylum claims in an effort to discourage immigrants from filing fraudulent petitions.

1995   The Commission on Immigration Reform, a bipartisan federal advisory panel, recommended a gradual reduction in legal immigration by one-third to a level of 550,000 a year from 830,000 a year.

1996   President Clinton signed into law the Illegal Immigration Reform and Immigrant Responsibility Act imposing new measures against "illegal immigration," which added agents to the Border Patrol and Immigration and Naturalization Service, and set a one-year time limit after entering the United States to applicants for political asylum.

1997   In reforms to the 1996 immigration law, Congress passed measures allowing hundreds of thousands of refugees from Central America and other regions to remain in the United States.

The U.S. Commission on Immigration Reform issued its final report to Congress, reiterating its 1995 endorsement of reductions in legal immigration while also giving its endorsement to legal immigration as a component of economic growth in the United States.

1998   Since passage of the Illegal Immigration Reform and Immigrant Responsibility Act in 1996, almost 300,000 immigrants were deported by federal authorities. The immigration act broadened the types of crimes committed by legal immigrants that would put them in a "criminal alien" category.

U.S. circuit courts in San Francisco and Boston struck down a provision of the immigration act that prohibited immigrants from fighting deportation or detainment in federal courts.

1999   The U.S. Supreme Court ruled that foreigners were ineligible for refugee protection in the United States if they committed a "serious nonpolitical crime" in their own country, regardless of whether they might face political persecution if deported.

2001   In the wake of the September 11 terrorist attacks on the United States, the number of refugees admitted to the United States declined as screening procedures were tightened and refugee resettlement programs were suspended.

Passage of the USA PATRIOT Act granted the government broad new powers for law enforcement and intelligence agencies to investigate and detain immigrants suspected of involvement in terrorism.

2002   The Department of Homeland Security was created through the merger of twenty-two U.S. government agencies, among them the Immigration and Naturalization Service, to prevent and respond to terrorism.

2003   The U.S. Supreme Court ruled that the 1996 Illegal Immigration Reform and Immigrant Responsibility Act's ban on deportation-order appeals for convicted aliens did not cover habeas corpus petitions.

2005   The proportion of legal immigrants who have become naturalized U.S. citizens reached its highest level in twenty-five years, a total of 12.8 million.

2006   The issue of immigration reform generated rallies and protests in cities across the United States, largely in support of granting undocumented immigrants some type of legal status.

2010   The Development, Relief, and Education for Alien Minors Act (DREAM Act) failed to pass the Senate by five votes, despite passage in the House. This legislation would have provided protection against deportation to children who arrived in the United States while under the age of 16 and with parents who were undocumented. Pending meeting certain criteria, these children would have a pathway to citizenship.

2011   The Obama administration released a "Blueprint
              for Building a 21st Century Immigration Sys-
              tem." This outlined ways to address deficiencies
              in the current immigration system and to im-
              prove the system to meet the country's economic
              and security needs and maintain its tradition of
              valuing the law and contributions of immigrants.
              The administration cited its enhanced security
              measures, but emphasized the necessity, for ex-
              ample, of welcoming smart individuals who start
              companies and generate jobs and of ensuring
              employers do not exploit undocumented workers
              and have access to means of verifying the legal
              status of employees. Reuniting immigrant fami-
              lies and developing pathways with the appropri-
              ate checks and requirements for legal status and
              citizenship were all critical to this vision.

2012   As a stopgap measure when the DREAM Act
              was stalled in Congress, President Obama is-
              sued through executive action Deferred Action
              for Childhood Arrivals (DACA). This program
              enabled undocumented immigrants, who ar-
              rived in the United States before they turned
              16 and who met certain criteria, to live in the
              country free from fear of deportation for a pe-
              riod of two years, subject to renewal. It also
              granted these individuals, known as Dreamers,
              eligibility for work authorization.

2013   The bipartisan Gang of 8 senators introduced the
              Border Security, Economic Opportunity, and

Immigration Modernization Act. The Senate passed this comprehensive immigration reform, but it was not voted on in the House. The major features of the legislation would have enhanced border security, improved the legal immigration process and visa and green card systems, and created a pathway to citizenship that would take up to 13 years for undocumented immigrants.

2013   A report by the Department of Homeland Security revealed a record number of deportations of undocumented immigrants during the fiscal year of 2013. Deportations surged by more than 20,000 over 2012 figures and by more than 50,000 over 2011.

2014   President Obama delivered a speech at a Las Vegas high school, outlining his steps of action to improve the immigration system since Congress failed to pass legislation on the issue. Obama authorized increased resources to law enforcement for enhanced border security, facilitation of access for high-skilled immigrants to remain in the country and protection from deportation, and a temporary stay for immigrants who met certain criteria.

2014   In a prime time speech, President Obama announced his executive action that granted parents of U.S. citizens and legal residents the ability to apply for temporary deportation deferrals and a work permit, if they have lived in the United States at least five years. In addition, he widened the eligibility requirements for recipients of DACA, opening up the program to immigrants older than the 2012 cutoff and who had arrived more recently to the country.

2016   Donald Trump accepted the Republican Party nomination for president and during his speech at the July Republican National Convention he cited his campaign promise to build a wall along the U.S.-Mexico border.

During his campaign, Trump stated in 2015, "When Mexico sends its people, they're not sending their best—they're not sending you . . . They're bringing drugs. They're bringing crime. They're rapists. And some, I assume, are good people."

January 2017   Less than a month after his inauguration, President Trump issued an executive order which barred citizens of 7 predominantly Muslim countries—Iran, Iraq, Libya, Somalia, Sudan, Syria, and Yemen—from entering the United States for 90 days. It also halted all refugee admission to the United States for 120 days and banned entry for Syrian refugees indefinitely. Protests erupted across the country and some federal judges immediately blocked parts of the order. The administration attempted to propose three additional iterations after federal courts stepped in to block them. The U.S. Supreme Court upheld the third version in June 2018.

February 2017	Immigrants, both undocumented and naturalized citizens throughout the country, designated a "Day Without Immigrants," refusing to work, operate their business, attend school, or shop. They demonstrated their impact on the economy and took a stand against Trump's immigration policies.
July 2017	Co-sponsored by a bipartisan group of senators, the Dream Act of 2017, which became known as the "clean" Dream Act, would provide a pathway to citizenship for DACA recipients and undocumented immigrants who met certain criteria and were under age 18 upon arrival to the United States.
August 2017	The Reforming American Immigration for Strong Employment (RAISE) Act was introduced in the Senate. The legislation proposed to reduce by half the number of legal immigrants permitted into the country to 500,000, establish a fiscal year limit of 50,000 refugees eligible for permanent residency, and refocus visa allotment to the nuclear family and to be merit and skill-based.
September 2017	Announcing his intention to begin phasing out DACA in six months, President Trump gave Congress until March 5, 2018 to create a new program. Congress could not agree on a plan by the deadline, but federal judges ruled against the President's decision to terminate DACA. Its future remains in limbo.

January   The White House announced its framework
2018   on immigration and border security. The plan
               would include a 10- to 12-year pathway to citi-
               zenship for DACA recipients and those eligible
               for the program, but who had not applied. In
               addition, it would terminate the visa lottery and
               limit immigration sponsorship to the nuclear
               family. A $25 billion trust fund would contrib-
               ute to the cost of a border wall and other se-
               curity measures would be enacted, including an
               increase of U.S. Immigration and Customs En-
               forcement (ICE) and Department of Homeland
               Security (DHS) personnel and stricter vigilance
               on removing individuals residing in the United
               States without documentation or valid visas.

March   The U.S. Department of Commerce, prompted
2018   by a request from the Department of Justice,
               announced the insertion of a citizenship status
               question on the 2020 decennial census. Mul-
               tiple lawsuits have been filed including by at-
               torneys general from 18 states against officials
               at the Department of Commerce and the U.S.
               Census Bureau.

May 2018   Attorney General Jeff Sessions announced an ex-
               panded "zero tolerance" policy toward migrants
               crossing the U.S.-Mexico border. Attorney Gen-
               eral Sessions committed to separating minors
               from their parents and referring anyone without
               documentation for criminal prosecution. This re-
               sulted in thousands of children being separated

from their parents and a humanitarian crisis at
the border. In June 2018, federal courts halted the
Administration's practice of family separations at
the border, ordered the Administration to implement reunification, and blocked the Administration from indefinitely detaining children.

At the time of publication, many aspects of federal immigration policies were under review by courts of various levels. By the summer of 2018, protests had taken place all over
the country in favor of reinstating protections and rights for
immigrants, refugees, asylum-seekers, and migrant families.
U.S. District Courts continued to intervene to block federal
anti-immigrant policies and uphold the principles of fairness
and just treatment upon which the country stands.

Appendix C

SUGGESTED READING

The following bibliography is in no way inclusive, but are suggestions of titles for further learning about immigration issues in the United States.

GENERAL

https://www.adl.org/education-and-resources

Bahrampour, Tara. *To See And See Again: A Life in Iran and America*. Berkeley and Los Angeles: University of California Press, 2000. The story of several generations of a family originally from Iran focusing on their experiences dealing with different expectations of each generation.

Beard, Annie E. S. *Our Foreign-Born Citizens*. New York: Crowell, 1922. Short biographies of well-known Americans of foreign birth.

Bernard, William S., et al., eds. *American Immigration Policy*. New York: Harper, 1950. Describes the origins and effects of the quota system.

Bruce, Campbell J. *The Golden Door*. New York: Random House, 1954. Case studies of the present effects of immigration and deportation policies.

Clark III, Louis V. *How to Be an Indian in the 21st Century*. Madison, WI: Wisconsin Historical Society Press, 2017. This book focuses on the struggles Clark faced in trying to maintain his heritage.

Coan, Peter Morton. *Toward a Better Life*. New York: Prometheus Books, 2011. Various immigrants tell their stories in their own words.

Cole, Stewart G., and Cole, Mildred Wiese. *Minorities and the American Promise*. New York: Harper, 1954. Discusses the relations of 180 million Americans of many racial, religious and national stocks.

Commager, Henry Steele, ed. *Immigration and American History*. Minneapolis: University of Minnesota Press, 1961. Essays discussing a number of aspects of American immigration.

Corsi, Edward. *In the Shadow of Liberty*. New York: Macmillan, 1935. The story of Ellis Island told by the first United States Commissioner of Immigration.

Divine, Robert A. *American Immigration Policy, 1924–1952*. New Haven: Yale, 1957. A comprehensive treatment of immigration policy.

Eaton, Allen H. *Immigrant Gifts to American Life*. New York: Russell Sage Foundation, 1932. Contributions of our foreign-born citizens to American cultural development.

Glazer, Nathan, and Moynihan, Daniel. *Beyond the Melting Pot*. Cambridge: M.I.T., 1963. Negroes, Puerto Ricans, Jews, Italians and Irish of New York City.

Guillet, Edwin C. *The Great Migration: The Atlantic Crossing by Sailing Ship Since 1770*. New York: Nelson, 1937. Dramatic description of conditions in port cities at both ends of the immigrant journey and aboard ship.

Handlin, Oscar. *The Americans*. Boston: Little, Brown, 1963. Discusses the gradual unfolding of the American character.

_____ (ed.). *Immigration as a Factor in American History*. New York: Spectrum Books, Prentice-Hall, 1959.

_____ (ed.). *This Was America*. Cambridge: Harvard, 1949 (Harper Torchbooks). True accounts as recorded by European travelers in the eighteenth, nineteenth and twentieth centuries.

_____. *The Uprooted*. Boston: Atlantic Monthly Press, 1951 (Universal Library). The story of the great migrations that made the American people.

Hansen, Marcus Lee. *The Atlantic Migration, 1607–1860*. Cambridge: Harvard, 1940 (Harper Torchbooks). The origins and transfer of immigrants from Europe to the United States.

_____. *The Immigrant in American History*. Cambridge: Harvard, 1940 (Harper Torchbooks). Interpretive essays on the immigration contribution.

Hendricks, Tyche. *The Wind Doesn't Need A Passport*. Berkeley and Los Angeles: University of California Press, 2010. A story of life on the U.S.-Mexico border.

Higham, John. *Strangers in the Land.* New Brunswick: Rutgers, 1955 (Atheneum Paperbacks). Patterns of American nativism, 1860–1925.

Jaworski, Irene D. *Becoming American.* New York: Harper, 1960. Describes the various problems the immigrant encounters in adjusting to American life.

Jones, Maldwyn Allen. *American Immigration.* Chicago: University of Chicago Press, 1960. Traces the impact of immigrants on American culture, politics, and economic growth.

Maisel, Albert Q. *They All Chose America.* New York: Nelson, 1957. A popular account of the various nationalities who came to America.

Potter, George. *To the Golden Door.* Boston: Little, Brown, 1960. Story of the Irish in Ireland and America.

Riis, Jacob. *How the Other Half Lives.* New York: Charles Scribner's Sons, 1890. This book focuses on immigrants living in tenements.

Schermerhorn, R. A. *These Our People: Minorities in American Culture.* New York: Heath, 1949. One-chapter treatments of five immigrant groups: Italians, Poles, Czechs and Slovaks, Hungarians and Yugoslavians.

Schlesinger, Arthur M. *Paths to the Present.* New York: Macmillan, 1949 (Sentry Editions, Houghton Mifflin). Discusses various phases of immigration, including the role of the immigrant in shaping American ideals.

Senior, Clarence. *Strangers Then Neighbors: From Pilgrims to Puerto Ricans.* New York: Anti-Defamation League, 1961. Examines the pattern and history of immigration to the U.S., with emphasis on the significance of recent Puerto Rican migration.

Stephenson, George M. *A History of American Immigration— 1820–1924*. Boston: Ginn, 1926. A discussion of immigration as a factor in American political development.

Vargas, Jose Antonio. *Dear America: Notes of an Undocumented Citizen*. New York: Dey Street Books, 2018.

Wittke, Carl. *We Who Built America: The Saga of the Immigrant*. Cleveland: Western Reserve University Press, 1939. Storehouse of information on various aspects of immigration.

Woodham-Smith, Cecil. *The Great Hunger*. New York: Harper, 1963 (Signet Books). The conditions in Ireland that led to mass emigration to the United States.

Zolberg, Aristide R. *A Nation By Design: Immigration Policy in the Fashioning of America*. Cambridge: First Harvard University Press, 2008. A review of American immigration policy and the factors that influenced it throughout the history of the country.

STUDIES IN SPECIALIZED AREAS

Abbott, Edith, ed. *Historical Aspects of the Immigration Problem*. Chicago: University of Chicago Press, 1926. Select documents relating to immigration.

Billington, Ray Allen. *The Protestant Crusade, 1800–1860: A Study of the Origins of American Nativism*. New York:

Macmillan, 1938 (Quadrangle Books). A study of anti-Catholic propaganda in the nineteenth century.

Blegen, Theodore C., ed. *Land of Their Choice: The Immigrants Write Home*. Minneapolis: University of Minnesota Press, 1955. Collection of letters of immigrants describing their life in this country.

Boorstin, Daniel J. *The Americans: The Colonial Experience*. New York: Random House, 1958. Impact of the American environment upon the various groups of colonists.

Childs, Frances S. *French Refugee Life in the United States, 1790–1800*. Baltimore: Johns Hopkins, 1940. Describes an American chapter of the French Revolution.

Craven, Wesley F. *The Legend of the Founding Fathers*. New York: New York University Press, 1956. Origins of the Puritan migrations.

Dunigan, Peter, and Gann, L. H. *The United States and Africa: A History*. New York: Cambridge University Press, 1984.

Erickson, Charlotte. *American Industry and the European Immigrant, 1860–1885*. Cambridge: Harvard, 1957. A study of the immigrants' effects on American industrialization.

Ernst, Robert. *Immigrant Life in New York City, 1825–1863*. New York: King's Crown Press, 1949. The intermingling of various groups during the mid-nineteenth century.

Foner, Nancy, ed. *Across Generations: Immigrant Families in America*. New York: New York University Press, 2009. A look at issues facing immigrant families living in the United States.

Gonzales, Manuel G. *Mexicanos, Second Edition: A History of Mexicans in the United States*. Bloomington, Indiana: Indiana University Press, 2009.

Hall, Matthew, Audrey Singer, Gordon F. De Jong, Deborah Roempke Graefe. *The Geography of Immigrant Skills: Education Profiles of Metropolitan Areas.* The Brooking Institute, June 2011. An analysis of the educational levels of adult immigrants in many large American cities.

Handlin, Oscar. *Danger in Discord.* New York: Anti-Defamation League, 1948. Origins of anti-Semitism in the United States.

_____. *Boston's Immigrants, 1790–1865; A Study in Acculturation.* Cambridge: Harvard, 1941. Describes the "Yankee" hostility to immigration in Boston.

Hirschman, Charles. *The Impact of Immigration on American Society: Looking Backward to the Future.* Institute for Human Sciences, 2007.

Janson, Florence Edith. *The Background of Swedish Immigration, 1840–1930.* Chicago: University of Chicago Press, 1931. The impulses which sent the Swedes to the United States.

Korn, Bertram Wallace. *American Jewry and the Civil War.* New York: Meridian Paperbacks, 1951. Includes a study of the outbreak of anti-Semitism during this period.

Marcus, Jacob R. *Early American Jewry.* Philadelphia: Jewish Publication Society, 1951. An account of the Jews in the colonial period in New York, New England and Canada.

Mulder, William. *Homeward to Zion.* Minneapolis: University of Minnesota Press, 1957. The Norman migration from Scandinavia.

Murray, Robert K. *Red Scare: A Study in National Hysteria, 1919–1920.* Minneapolis: University of Minnesota Press,

1955 (McGraw-Hill Paperback Series). Evaluation of the Palmer Raids and other manifestations of this period.

Nevins, Allan, and Hill, Frank E. *Ford: Expansion and Challenge* (2nd volume of a 3-volume work). New York: Scribner, 1957. Covers Ford's venture into anti-Semitism.

Nunn, Nathan, Nancy Qian, Sandra Sequeira. *Does Immigration Help or Hurt Local Economies?* Kellogg Insight, Northwestern University, 2017. This research study suggests that immigration leads to prosperity.

Penn Wharton, University of Pennsylvania. *The Effect of Immigration on the United States' Economy*, 2016.

Phillips, Ulrich Bonnell. *American Negro Slavery.* Gloucester: Peter Smith, 1959. A discussion of aspects of the slave trade.

Rischin, Moses. *The Promised City.* Cambridge: Harvard, 1962. Jewish community life in New York City, 1870–1914.

Saloutos, Theodore. *They Remember America.* Berkeley: University of California Press, 1956. The story of repatriated Greek-Americans.

Sandmeyer, Elmer C. *The Anti-Chinese Movement in California.* Urbana: University of Illinois Press, 1939. Traces the growth of nativism in California.

Schrier, Arnold. *Ireland and American Emigration, 1850–1900.* Minneapolis: University of Minnesota Press, 1958. American influences which filtered back to Ireland.

Smith, Abbott E. *Colonists in Bondage: White Servitude and Convict Labor in America, 1607–1776.* Chapel Hill: University of North Carolina Press, 1947. A treatment of the problem of indentured servants who came to America.

Smith, James Morton. *Freedom's Fetters*. Ithaca: Cornell University Press, 1956. The Alien and Sedition Acts and American civil liberties.

Solomon, Barbara. *Ancestors and Immigrants*. Cambridge: Harvard, 1956. A study of New England nativism.

Tupper, Eleanor, and McReynolds, George E. *Japan in American Public Opinion*. New York: Macmillan, 1937. Traces American antipathies to Japanese migration.

Wittke, Carl F. *The German-Language Press in America*. Lexington: University of Kentucky Press, 1957. The influence of German newspapers on American life.

————. *Refugees of Revolution: The German Forty-Eighters in America*. Philadelphia: University of Pennsylvania Press, 1952. A study of the people who fled Germany at the time of the revolutions of 1848.

MINORITIES IN AMERICA

Berthoff, Rowland T. *British Immigrants in Industrial America, 1790–1950*. Cambridge: Harvard, 1953.

Bixler, Mark. *The Lost Boys of Sudan. An American Story of the Refugee Experience*. Athens, GA: The University of Georgia Press, 2005. This is a story about four refugees from Sudan and their experiences coming to and living in the United States.

Blegen, Theodore C. *Norwegian Migration to America, 1825–1860*. Northfield, Minn.: Norwegian-American History Association, 1940.

Burma, John H. *Spanish-Speaking Groups in the United States.* Durham: Duke, 1954.

Conway, Alan, ed. *The Welsh in America; Letters from Immigrants.* Minneapolis: University of Minnesota Press, 1961.

Davis, Jerome D. *The Russian Immigrant.* New York: Macmillan, 1922.

Faust, Albert B. *The German Element in the United States.* 2 vols. New York: Houghton, 1909.

Foerster, Robert F. *The Italian Emigration of Our Times.* Cambridge: Harvard, 1919.

Fosdick, Lucian J. *The French Blood in America.* Baltimore: Genealogical Publishing Company, 1973.

Ginzberg, Eli, and Eichner, Alfred S. *The Troublesome Presence: American Democracy and the Negro.* New York: Free Press, 1964.

Govorchin, G. G. *Americans from Yugoslavia.* Gainesville: University of Florida Press, 1961.

Graham, Ian. *Colonists from Scotland.* Ithaca: Cornell University Press, 1956.

Handlin, Oscar. *Adventure in Freedom.* New York: McGraw-Hill, 1954. Discusses three hundred years of Jewish life in America.

Hansen, Marcus Lee. *The Mingling of the Canadian and American Peoples.* New Haven: Yale, 1940.

Hawgood, John A. *The Tragedy of German-America; The Germans in the United States of America during the Nineteenth Century—and After.* Toronto: T. Allen, 1940.

Hitti, Philip K. *The Syrians in America.* New York: George H. Doran, 1924.

Hoglund, William A. *Finnish Immigrants in America.* Madison: University of Wisconsin Press, 1960.

Hsu, Madeline T. *The Good Immigrants: How the Yellow Peril Became the Model Minority.* Princeton and Oxford: Princeton University Press, 2015.

Ichihashi, Yamato. *Japanese in the United States.* Stanford: Stanford University Press, 1932.

Learsi, Rufus. *The Jews in America: A History.* Cleveland: World, 1954.

Lee, Erika. *The Making of Asian America: A History.* New York: Simon and Schuster, 2015.

Lee, Rose Hum. *The Chinese in the United States of America.* London: Oxford, 1960.

Lengyel, Emil. *Americans from Hungary.* Philadelphia: Lippincott, 1948.

Leyburn, James, *The Scotch-Irish: A Social History.* Chapel Hill: University of North Carolina Press, 1962.

Lucas, Henry S. *Netherlanders in America.* Ann Arbor: University of Michigan Press, 1955.

Malcolm, M. Varton. *The Armenians in America.* Boston: Pilgrim Press, 1919.

Mcwilliams, Carey. *North from Mexico.* Westport, CT: Greenwood Press, 1990.

Mills, Senior, Kohn and Goldsen. *The Puerto Rican Journey.* New York: Harper, 1950.

Regan, Margaret. *The Death of Josseline: Immigration Stories from the Arizona-Mexico borderlands.* Boston: Beacon Press, 2010.

Reid, Ira De Augustine. *The Negro Immigrant, His Background, Characteristics, and Social Adjustment.* New York: Columbia, 1939.

Saloutos, Theodore. *The Greeks in the U.S.* Cambridge: Harvard, 1964.

Shannon, William V. *The American Irish.* New York: Macmillan, 1963.

Smith, Bradford. *Americans from Japan.* Philadelphia: Lippincott, 1948.

Wittke, Carl F. *The Irish in America.* Baton Rouge: Louisiana State, 1956.

Wytrwal, Joseph A. *America's Polish Heritage.* Detroit: Endurance Press, 1961.

APPENDIX D

TEXT OF PRESIDENT JOHN F. KENNEDY'S PROPOSALS TO LIBERALIZE IMMIGRATION STATUTES

(JULY 23, 1963)

I AM TRANSMITTING HEREWITH, FOR THE CONSIDER-ation of the Congress, legislation revising and modernizing our immigration laws. More than a decade has elapsed since the last substantial amendment to these laws. I believe there exists a compelling need for the Congress to reexamine and make certain changes in these laws.

The most urgent and fundamental reform I am recommending relates to the national origins system of selecting immigrants. Since 1924 it has been used to determine the number of quota immigrants permitted to enter the United States each year. Accordingly, although the legislation I am transmitting deals with many problems which require remedial action, it concentrates attention primarily upon revision of our quota immigration system. The enactment of this legislation will not resolve all of our important problems in the field of immigration law. It will, however, provide a sound basis upon which we can build in developing an immigration law that serves the national interest and reflects in every detail the principles of equality and human dignity to which our nation subscribes.

ELIMINATION OF DISCRIMINATION BASED ON NATIONAL ORIGINS

Present legislation establishes a system of annual quotas to govern immigration from each country. Under this system, 156,700 quota immigrants are permitted to enter the United States each year. The system is based upon the national origins of the population of the United States in 1920. The use of the year 1920 is arbitrary. It rests upon the fact that this system was introduced in 1924 and the last prior census was in 1920. The use of a national origins system is without basis in either logic or reason. It neither satisfies a national need nor accomplishes an international purpose. In an age of interdependence among nations, such a system is an anachronism, for it discriminates among applicants for admission into the United States on the basis of accident of birth.

Because of the composition of our population in 1920, the system is heavily weighted in favor of immigration from Northern Europe and severely limits immigration from Southern and Eastern Europe and from other parts of the world. An American citizen with a Greek father or mother must wait at least eighteen months to bring his parents here to join him. A citizen whose married son or daughter, or brother or sister, is Italian cannot obtain a quota number for an even longer time. Meanwhile, many thousands of quota numbers are wasted because they are not wanted or needed by nationals of the countries to which they are assigned.

I recommend that there be substituted for the national origins system a formula governing immigration to the United States which takes into account (1) the skills of the immigrant and their relationship to our need; (2) the family relationship between immigrants and persons already here, so that the reuniting of families is encouraged and (3) the priority of registration. Present law grants a preference to immigrants with special skills, education or training. It also grants a preference to various relatives of United States citizens and lawfully resident aliens. But it does so only within a national origins quota. It should be modified so that those with the greatest ability to add to the national welfare, no matter where they were born, are granted the highest priority. The next priority should go to those who seek to be reunited with their relatives. As between applicants with equal claims the earliest registrant should be the first admitted.

Many problems of fairness and foreign policy are involved in replacing a system so long entrenched. The national origins system has produced large backlogs of applications in some countries, and too rapid a change might, in a system of limited immigration, so drastically curtail immigration in some countries the only effect might be to shift the unfairness from one group of nations to another. A reasonable time to adjust to any new system must be provided if individual hardships upon persons who were relying on the present system are to be avoided. In addition, any new system must have sufficient flexibility to allow adjustments to be made when it appears that immigrants from nations closely allied to the United States will be unduly restricted in their freedom to furnish the new seed population that has so long been a source of strength to our nation.

PROPOSAL IN DETAIL

Accordingly, I recommend:

First, that existing quotas be reduced gradually, at the rate of 20 percent a year. The quota numbers released each year would be placed in a quota reserve pool, to be distributed on the new basis.

Second, that natives of no one country receive over 10 percent of the total quota numbers authorized in any one year. This will insure that the pattern of immigration is not distorted by excessive demand from any one country.

Third, that the President be authorized, after receiving recommendations from a seven-man Immigration Board, to reserve up to 50 percent of the unallocated quota numbers for issuance to persons disadvantaged by the change in the quota system, and up to 20 percent to refugees whose sudden dislocation requires special treatment. The Immigration Board will be composed of two members appointed by the Speaker of the House of Representatives, two members appointed by the President Pro Tempore of the Senate, and three members appointed by the President. In addition to its responsibility for formulating recommendations regarding the use of the quota reserve pool, the Board will make a continuous study of our immigration policy.

ALL QUOTA NUMBERS USED

But it is not alone the initial assignment of quota numbers which is arbitrary and unjust; additional inequity results from the failure of the law to permit full utilization of the authorized quota numbers. While American citizens wait for years for their relatives to receive a quota, approximately sixty thousand quota numbers are wasted each year because the countries to which they are assigned have far more numbers allocated to them than they have emigrants seeking to move to the United States. There is no way at present in which these numbers can be reassigned to nations where immense backlogs of applicants for admission to the United States have accumulated. I recommend that this deficiency in the law be corrected.

ASIA-PACIFIC TRIANGLE

A special discriminatory formula is now used to regulate the immigration of persons who are attributable by their ancestry to an area called the Asia-Pacific triangle. This area embraces all countries from Pakistan to Japan and the Pacific islands north of Australia and New Zealand. Usually, the quota under which a prospective immigrant must enter is determined by his place of birth. However, if as much as one-half of an immigrant's ancestors came from nations in the Asia-Pacific triangle, he must rely upon the small quota assigned to the country of his ancestry, regardless of where he was born. This provision of our law should be repealed.

OTHER PROVISIONS

In order to remove other existing barriers to the reuniting of families, I recommend two additional improvements in the law.

First, parents of American citizens, who now have a preferred quota status, should be accorded nonquota status.

Second, parents of aliens resident in the United States, who now have no preference, should be accorded a preference, after skilled specialists and other relatives of citizens and alien residents.

These changes will have little effect on the number of immigrants admitted. They will have a major effect upon the individual hardships many of our citizens and residents now face in being separated from their parents.

In addition, I recommend the following changes in the law in order to correct certain deficiencies and improve its general application.

1. Changes in the Preference Structure. At present, the procedure under which specially skilled or trained workers are permitted to enter this country too often prevents talented people from applying for visas to enter the United States. It often deprives us of immigrants who would be helpful to our economy and our culture. This procedure should be liberalized so that highly trained or skilled persons may obtain a preference without requiring that they secure employment here before emigrating. In addition, I recommend that a special preference be accorded workers with lesser skills who can fill specific needs in short supply in this country.

2. <u>Nonquota status for natives of Jamaica, Trinidad and Tobago should be granted.</u> Under existing law, no numerical limitation is imposed upon the number of immigrants coming from Canada, Mexico, Cuba, Haiti, the Dominican Republic, the Canal Zone or any independent country in Central or South America. But the language of the statute restricts this privilege to persons born in countries in the Caribbean area which gained their independence prior to the date of the last major amendment to the immigration and nationality statutes, in 1952. This accidental discrimination against the newly independent nations of the Western Hemisphere should be corrected.

3. <u>Persons afflicted with mental health problems should be admitted provided certain standards are met.</u> Today, any person afflicted with a mental disease or mental defect, psychotic personality, or epilepsy, and any person who has suffered an attack of mental illness, can enter this country only if a private bill is enacted for his benefit. Families which are able and willing to care for a mentally ill child or parent are often forced to choose between living in the United States and leaving their loved ones behind and not living in the United States but being able to see and care for their loved ones. Mental illness is not incurable. It should be treated like other illnesses. I recommend that the Attorney General, at his discretion and under proper safeguards, be authorized to waive those provisions of the law which prohibit the admission to the United States of persons with mental problems when they are close relatives of United States citizens and lawfully resident aliens.

4. <u>The Secretary of State should be authorized, in his discretion, to require re-registration of certain quota immigrant</u>

<u>visa applicants and to regulate the time of payment of visa fees.</u> This authority would bring registration lists up to date, terminate the priority of applicants who have refused to accept a visa, and end the problem of "insurance" registrations by persons who have no present intention to emigrate. Registration figures for oversubscribed quota areas are now inaccurate because there exists no way of determining whether registrants have died, have emigrated to other countries, or for some other reason no longer want to emigrate to the United States. These problems are particularly acute in heavily oversubscribed areas.

CONCLUSION

As I have already indicated the measures I have outlined will not solve all the problems of immigration. Many of them will require additional legislation; some cannot be solved by any one country. But the legislation I am submitting will insure that progress will continue to be made toward our ideals and toward the realization of humanitarian objectives. The measures I have recommended will help eliminate discrimination between peoples and nations on a basis that is unrelated to any contribution that immigrants can make and is inconsistent with our traditions of welcome. Our investment in new citizens has always been a valuable source of our strength.

Appendix E

SELECTED COMMENTS ON PRESIDENT KENNEDY'S MESSAGE

Senator Philip A. Hart, Democrat of Michigan, speaking of the message on revision of the immigration laws sent to the Congress in 1963, said:

It is fitting that this proposal should come at a time when the nation and the Congress are deeply committed to a full review of our practices and laws affecting our fellow citizens of different races. . . . Let us get on with this job.

From the other side of the chamber, Republican Senator Kenneth B. Keating of New York declared:

I am very pleased that the executive branch has now made these proposals and I am sympathetic to the approach in this bill. . . . I shall certainly exert every possible effort to have such legislation enacted at this session . . . and hope that there will be prompt hearings on this important subject.

Strong support for a thoroughgoing revision of our present immigration policy came from Senator Hubert H. Humphrey, the Minnesota Democrat. He said:

Although Congress faces many urgent matters of national importance at this session and the next, I fervently hope we can nevertheless push ahead with the long-postponed, long-overdue task of bringing our immigration laws up to the civilized standard which the world has reason to expect of the United States. The present system is cruel, unworkable, discriminatory, and illogical.

Republican Senator Hiram L. Fong of Hawaii said: "I shall strongly support efforts to basically revise our immigration laws and policies," and added that he was "heartened" by the administration's recognition of the need for a basic change in American immigration policies.

Congressman Emanuel Celler of New York, Chairman of the House Judiciary Committee, said:

It is my considered opinion that the President's bill offers a broad and firm basis for a long overdue revision of our policies and practices in this most important area of domestic and foreign human relations.

Congressman James Roosevelt of California stated:

The President of the United States has urgently called upon the Congress to implement long overdue and sorely needed changes in our immigration laws.

I would like to strongly urge my colleagues to join with me in supporting this new and far reaching immigration proposal of the President's.

Congressman William F. Ryan of New York said:

I believe that President Kennedy's proposals represent a giant step forward in the creation of a sensible and humane immigration policy.

Newspaper editorials reflected a similar, nonpartisan approach to the projected revisions. The *Chicago Tribune* commented:

The idea of shifting the basis of immigrants' admission from the arbitrary one of country of origin to the rational and humane ones of occupational skills and reuniting families deserves approval.

The policy of action without regard to race, religion, or country of origin has increasing appeal and scope in the United States, especially in the processes of government. The immigration quotas have been the principal exception in federal practice to equality before the law for people whatever the circumstances of their birth. It is an exception that it is well to reconsider.

The *Denver Post* approvingly said of the proposed changes:

It would replace a system based on racial and national discrimination with one having two worthwhile and humane
objectives: to assure the United States of a continuing flow
of usefully-skilled new citizens, and to reunite the families
of U.S. citizens.

The *Washington Post,* July 24, 1963, called President
Kennedy's proposal "the best immigration law within living
memory to bear a White House endorsement."

The *New York Times,* July 25, 1963, in its lead editorial stated:

. . . Adoption of the President's wise recommendations
would be an act of justice and wisdom, as well as evidence
that we fully understand the true nature of the changed
world—now grown so small—in which all humanity lives.

The *St. Paul Pioneer Press* editorialized on July 26, 1963:

Possibly the only negative feature of the administration's
new immigration plan is the five years it proposes to take
in implementing it. The present system is so archaic and
inflexible as to deserve speedier abandonment.

"It is time to lay aside the thinking of the '20s in favor
of the realities of the '60s with regard to our unreasonable
quota system on immigration," wrote the *Chattanooga Times.*
It continued:

The system of national quotas has long been recognized as a paradox, in a nation proud of its pattern of growth and development based in large part on the openness of its shores to people seeking an opportunity in the "land of opportunity."

The quota system was set up in the immigration law of 1924. Many of its supporters saw this as a means of checking an Asian immigration invasion. But others adapted it to meet their own desires to limit the number who could come to this country from Southern Europe.

We are a big nation with room—and a continuing need—to grow stronger. We can do this with the skill and ability of our native born and of those from other lands who wish to be a part of this great nation and to work with us in trying to fulfill its ideals.

The time to worry about immigration is when people stop wanting to come to this country.

Seventy-two leading religious, civic, labor and social service agencies, members of the American Immigration and Citizenship Conference, jointly commended the President as follows:

We wish to endorse strongly the historic step you have taken in your Message of July 23 in calling for the elimination of the National Origins Quota System.

We have long urged the removal of this discriminatory aspect of our American immigration policy.

We are greatly encouraged and wish to express our appreciation for the outstanding leadership you are giving in this major field of human rights.

APPENDIX F

INTRODUCTION TO THE
2008 EDITION

by Edward M. Kennedy

My brother Jack wrote *A Nation of Immigrants* in 1958, and his words ring true as clearly today as they did half a century ago. No one spoke more eloquently about our history and heritage as a nation of immigrants or fought harder on behalf of fair and rational immigration laws than President Kennedy.

One of his last acts as president was to propose a major series of immigration reforms to end the ugly race-based national origins quota system, which had defined our admissions policies in that era. As he told Congress in July of 1963: "The enactment of this legislation will not resolve all of our important problems in the field of immigration law. It will, however, provide a sound basis upon which we can build in developing an immigration law that serves the national interest and reflects in every detail the principles of equality and human dignity to which our nation subscribes."

A century and a half ago, all eight of our Irish great-grandparents successfully crossed the Atlantic in the famous vessels that were known as "coffin ships" because so many people failed to survive the arduous voyage. They arrived in Boston Harbor, came up the "Golden Stairs" and passed through the city's Immigration Hall on their way to a better life for themselves and their families. From my office in Boston, I can still see those "Golden Stairs," and I'm constantly reminded of my immigrant heritage.

As President Kennedy put it, "This was the secret of America: a nation of people with the fresh memory of old traditions who dared to explore new frontiers, people eager to build lives for themselves in a spacious society that did not restrict their freedom of choice and action."

Immigration is in our blood. It's part of our founding story. In the early 1600s, courageous men and women sailed in search of freedom and a better life. Arriving in Jamestown and Plymouth, they founded a great nation. For centuries ever since, countless other brave men and women have made the difficult decision to leave their homes and seek better lives in this promised land.

In New York Harbor, there stands a statue that represents the enduring ideal of what has made this nation great—a beacon on a hill. At her feet, on the pedestal on which the Statue of Liberty stands, are inscribed the eloquent words of poet Emma Lazarus:

> Give me your tired, your poor,
> Your huddled masses yearning to breathe free,
> The wretched refuse of your teeming shore.

Send these, the homeless, tempest-tost to me,
I lift my lamp beside the golden door!

Immigrants today come from all corners of the world, representing every race and creed. They work hard. They practice their faith. They love their families. And they love this country. We would not be a great nation today without them. But whether we remain true to that history and heritage is a major challenge.

There is no question that the immigration system needs to be reformed to meet the challenges of the twenty-first century. The urgent issue before us is about the future of America. It is about being proud of our immigrant past and our immigrant future. We know the high price of continuing inaction. Raids and other enforcement actions will escalate, terrorizing our communities and businesses. The twelve million undocumented immigrants now in our country will become millions more. Sweatshops will grow and undermine American workers and their wages. State and local governments will take matters into their own hands and pass a maze of conflicting laws that hurt our country. We will have the kind of open border that is unacceptable in our post-9/11 world.

Immigration reform is an opportunity to be true to our ideals as a nation. At the heart of the issue of immigration is hope. Hope for a better life for hard-working people and their families. Hope for their children. Martin Luther King Jr. had a dream that children would be judged solely by "the content of their character." That dream will never die. I believe that we will soon succeed in enacting the kind of reform that our ideals and national security demand.

As we continue the battle, we will have ample inspiration in the lives of the immigrants all around us. From Jamestown to the Pilgrims to the Irish to today's workers, people have come to this country in search of opportunity. They have sought nothing more than the chance to work hard and build a better life for themselves and their families. They come to our country with their hearts and minds full of hope. I believe we can build the kind of tough, fair and practical reform that is worthy of our shared history as immigrants and as Americans.

With these challenges in mind, I commend this volume. Written five decades ago, its powerful vision still guides us.

ACKNOWLEDGMENTS

I T ' S   A N   I N T E R E S T I N G   T A S K   T O   T R Y   T O   P R E P A R E   A   S E T   O F acknowledgments for a book written 60 years ago by a former president. And yet, it does seem important to note those people past and present who helped to make this new edition possible.

First, let me extend my gratitude to Steven Rothstein and everyone at the John F. Kennedy Presidential Library and Museum who originally proposed the reprint. They are entrusted with guarding JFK's legacy and do so with dignity and grace. I am humbled that they believe that ADL remains the right partner to continue delivering this message, even 60 years later. Thank you to Congressman Joe Kennedy for honoring his great-uncle's inspiring dedication to immigration reform and for partnering with ADL. I also want to thank our friends at HarperCollins for their patience and support in undertaking this commemorative reprint. Their commitment made it possible.

I want to thank the team at ADL who worked on the reprint, particularly Amy Golod, who tirelessly managed this project from start to finish, always with a smile and with incredible attention to detail. Amy Blumkin ensured that the finished product reflected our modern identity without losing the thread of our timeless legacy. Steve Freeman and Melissa Garlick provided critical guidance on the policy issues related to immigration. Robert Trestan maintains and strengthens ADL's ties to the community of New England, home to generations of the Kennedy family. Emily Bromberg kept the project at the top of our priorities despite many other equally worthy items that could have gotten our attention.

Beyond this group, I am thankful to the extraordinary team of dedicated professionals who work at ADL and lead the fight against hate every single day. I am constantly inspired by their boundless energy and relentless fortitude. I also appreciate the support of the remarkable volunteers who elevate this work with their enthusiasm, ideas and resources. In particular, I want to acknowledge the past and present ADL chairs who I have served, but especially—Barry Curtiss-Lusher, Marvin Nathan and Esta Epstein. I am better for their leadership and smarter for their wisdom.

Finally, I am grateful to the leaders who came before me at ADL, the professional staff who laid the groundwork for the modern ADL. This includes our founder Sigmund Livingston; national directors including Leon Lewis, Dick Gutstadt, Nate Perlmutter and Abe Foxman; past regional directors such as Sheldon Steinhauser, A. I. "B" Botnick and the late Lenny Zakim, who first gave me a shot as an ADL intern in 1991. I particularly want to recognize Ben Epstein, the legendary leader who truly pioneered the modern ADL.

Ben went after anti-Semites and waged war on those who threatened the Jewish community. He advocated for the embattled state of Israel shortly after it was founded and helped to block the Arab Boycott that threatened to suffocate the fledgling country. But, long before it was fashionable, Ben also took a range of bold positions beyond the traditional Jewish remit—on school desegregation, on voting rights and on equal treatment under the law. And it was Ben who personally reached out to a junior senator from Massachusetts in 1957 with the idea of writing the piece that you now hold in your hands. More than anyone, Ben exemplified the spirit of Hillel and demonstrated that ADL could fight for the Jewish people and also fight for all people. He cemented our status as a modern civil rights organization and helped to ensure that, time and again, ADL landed on the right side of history.

Finally, I want to thank my wife, Marjan Keypour Greenblatt. A political refugee herself, she and her family escaped trauma and violence in the Middle East to be here in America. Her courage inspires me and her love keeps me going every day.

ALSO BY
JOHN F. KENNEDY

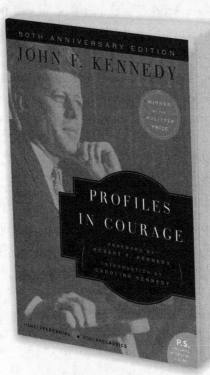

PROFILES IN COURAGE

Available in Hardcover, Paperback, eBook, CD, and Digital Audiobook

The Pulitzer Prize winning classic by President John F. Kennedy, with an introduction by Caroline Kennedy and a foreword by Robert F. Kennedy.

Written in 1955 by the then junior senator from the state of Massachusetts, John F. Kennedy's *Profiles in Courage* serves as a clarion call to every American. The book remains a moving, powerful, and relevant testament to the indomitable national spirit and an unparalleled celebration of that most noble of human virtues. It resounds with timeless lessons on the most cherished of virtues and is a powerful reminder of the strength of the human spirit.